QUALITY CIRCLE

LEADER MANUAL AND INSTRUCTIONAL GUIDE

By
Donald L. Dewar

QUALITY CIRCLE INSTITUTE
234 SOUTH MAIN STREET
RED BLUFF, CALIFORNIA 96080 U.S.A.

ISBN 0-937670-02-2

Illustrations by Steve Ferchaud

INTRODUCTION

As a team leader, you are one of the most important parts of a "movement" that is destined to change the work-life of millions of people.

You will guide a gathering of individuals who have heard enough about this new concept to make them want to meet with you to learn mmore about it. The knowledge that you will help them to gain will transform them into a highly skilled team that can perform with an expertise and precision that is difficult to believe until you see it in action.

The techniques that you will teach are

effective enough to enable your people to quickly gather essential data, evaluate it, and put it to use so skillfully -- so logically -- that management will not only listen to their recommendations, but will encourage them to make more.

You will see a marked improvement in communication. You will become aware that your people tend to prevent problems whenever possible, and overall morale will improve significantly. And, probably the most satisfying "side-effect" you will experience is that both you and the team you lead will get a tremendous amount of enjoyment out of this activity.

The teams that accomplish the most are the ones whose members have the most fun working together!

TABLE OF CONTENTS

SUGGESTED FORMS

GENERAL INFORMATION

You have probably already observed that this book contains some material which is printed in blue ink and some in red. The manuals which are supplied to members contain only that which is blue in this book. Nothing that is printed in red is included in their manuals; because the red part is written specifically for you.

In order to optimize communication between you concerning all of the training materials, your facilitator's manual contains everything that appears in this book.

There are nine chapters in the member manual,

the first of which is a series of questions and answers designed to reduce the amount of time you must devote to answering questions.

The balance of the manual ties in with eight A-V modules which you will use to train the members to do the various things that experience has proven to be essential to successful team operation.

Not knowing what your level of experience and expertise may be, the author has provided both some general suggestions for effective training and ten detailed meeting agendas to serve as a guide. In addition, there are suggestions for comments, explanations, and questions that you may want to use to stimulate member interest and involvement.

This kind of format necessarily calls for a certain amount of repetition; which you are sure to ignore as soon as you have established a routine of your own for getting the team leadership job done most effectively.

It is known that some leaders prefer to handle the the narration part of the training modules themselves; because it enables them to "customize" the training to more precisely fit their needs. Some do it because they can more easily adjust the rate of information flow to match the learning capacities of their groups. Again, depending upon your own preferences in such matters, you may want to do the same or to make some other alteration in how these modules are used. However, you can be certain that you will get highly satisfactory results by depending fully on both the audio and visual portions of these modules without any deviations of any kind. In fact, unskilled alterations should be avoided as they are likely to prove to be counter productive.

The member manual contains a substantial number of illustrations; but in the interest of avoiding excessive bulk and expense, not all of the pictures appearing in the A-V module are included. The small squares - □ - in the book indicate the existance of pictures in the visual module.

Preceding each chapter in the member manual, and following the last one, you will find material for your use.

The ten suggested meeting agendas contain

TABULATED SUGGESTED AGENDA

During Training	After Training	
X	X	Welcome members and guests
X	X	Introduce guests
X	X	Read and approve minutes
X		Review last lesson and re-do quiz, if needed
X		Discuss responses to worksheet exercise
X		Introduce the current lesson
X		Present the A-V module
X		Discuss the current lesson
X		Suggest completion of worksheet exercise
X	X	Work on a project
X	X	Give assignments, if appropriate
X	X	Post schedule and revise if needed
X	X	Suggest thinking about next project, or next phase of current one
X		Give quiz on current training module
X		Suggest members read about next lesson
X	X	Give date, time, and place of next meeting
X	X	Thank attendees for attention and co-operation
X	X	Make sure secretary prepares minutes
X	X	Confer with facilitator if required

numerous hints, some of which are for one-time use and others which are applicable to every meeting. On the next page you will find a check-list agenda for use while the members are being trained and after the initial training is completed. The word "initial" is used because you are sure to want to pursue an on-going training program by presenting the various modules whenever you sense the need to refresh the members' minds on a particular phase of the team activity.

BOTH THE LEADER AND MEMBER MANUALS HAVE BEEN DESIGNED TO PROVIDE EFFECTIVE MEMBER TRAINING WITH OR WITHOUT THE USE OF THE A-V MODULES. EVERY WORD CONTAINED IN THE AUDIO MODULE IS PRINTED IN THE MEMBER MANUAL. SOME OF THE PICTURES WHICH APPEAR IN THE VISUAL MODULE ARE PRINTED IN THE MEMBER MANUAL TO ILLUSTRATE SALIENT POINTS AND STIMULATE READER INTEREST.

GENERAL INSTRUCTIONAL SUGGESTIONS

The amount of time and attention you give to this part of your manual will depend upon your experience and knowledge; but, even if you are a teacher with top quality credentials, it is suggested that you read what follows, at least once.

Everything appearing in these manuals is included for a solid practical reason -- it has been proven to work. Teams that are implemented and operated according to these guidelines are successful. They are cost-effective. And the psychological effect on members results in a dramatic boost in morale with all the side-effects that go with it.

Training Aids

Prior to each meeting, be sure to arrange to have available whatever you will need for the efficient use of the time allotted. Here is a list to serve as a reminder:

The appropriate A-V training module

Audio-Visual equipment

Flip-chart, pad, easel, marking pens

Overhead projector

Blackboard, chalk, eraser

Opaque projector

35mm Projector

Giving Quizzes

In the suggested agendas, you will note that the training courses are given close to the beginning of each meeting and the quizzes are given shortly before the close. The atten- tion of the group may be focussed on a variety of subjects between the presentation of the current day's lesson and the quiz relating to it. This is done for the purpose of speeding up the learning process. The five distinct periods of concentration on each technique taught have proven to be beneficial -- (1) presentation of the A-V, (2) Quiz, (3) completion of worksheet exercise, (4) review of subject matter of lesson, and (5) discussion of completed worksheet exercises.

When giving the quizzes, avoid directing the questions to the members in turn; because they will tend to concentrate their attention only on the questions they know they will be called upon to answer. Read a question aloud before disclosing who is to answer it to assure that everyone remains alert and attentive; but try to be sure that everyone present is asked to answer at least one question. Employ the question, "Why is that?" often. It enhances understanding.

Worksheet Exercises

Team involvement is a voluntary activity, members are not required to do homework. However, they should be urged at every meeting to complete the worksheet exercises. After reviewing the previous meeting's training material, ask about

the worksheet exercises and discuss the members'
responses. This will almost surely result in
getting most of the members to complete them.
Explain that these exercises are a real learning
aid and should be taken seriously. They can help
the members to master the techniques to the
fullest possible degree.

Relate Training to Actual Work Situations

There's no better way to make what you are
teaching the members "real" than to relate what is
covered in the training modules to their actual
work situations. You may be better able to see
tie-ins than they are, but try to get them to
discover them on their own. Encourage them to
give lots of attention to doing this. It is a
very effective way to learn a new concept - a new
way of thinking. Members can become potent
sources for assuring tie-ins.

Robert's Rules of Order

Many occasions will present themselves when
you will be called upon to be an expert parlia-
mentarian. You will have to make order out of
chaos - particularly when member enthusiasm shifts
into high gear. This will be especially evident

when the voting takes place after a brainstorming session.

Members must always be encouraged to discuss items being voted on if they feel the need. Apply Robert's Rules of Order or any other applicable system at the meetings. Robert's rules were developed long ago, and they are designed to maintain order and provide a fair and equitable opportunity for all persons who participate in meetings.

"Stop the A-V!"

Your part of the manual indicates where the author believes the A-V should be stopped in order for you to reinforce understanding, emphasize certain points, point out tie-ins with actual on-the-job situations, and so on. This is important. It's easy for trainees to get their attention hung up on points that are unclear to them and thus get very little out of what transpires thereafter. As leader, you will be able, in many instances, to sense this occurance. Therefore, you are strongly urged to stop the A-V at any other points you feel necessary during the presentation. You are also urged to make it very clear to the members that their questions and comments and requests to stop the A-V are welcome at all times during the presentation of the training module. (This is one of the things we often remind you to do throughout this book. It's _that_ important!)

It takes two way communication to maximize the effectiveness of the training sessions. Encourage it!

An Enjoyable Experience

The group you lead has an excellent chance to be effective and successful because of the potential that's built into the activity. The concept is based on proven principles of the behavior and managerial sciences. But if the activity is an enjoyable experience both for you and your members, there is no visible limit to the success that can be attained! Make it fun! Draw people out! Get everyone involved! Give attainable assignments! Help the members and everyone they work with to _win_! There's a whole lot of potential in your group; and the concepts of employee participation will bring it out!

Each chapter of the member manual is reproduced in the following pages in blue ink.

The page numbers match those in the member manual for quick reference when required.

CHAPTER ONE

QUESTIONS & ANSWERS

WHAT IS IT?

A group of people who voluntarily meet together on a regular basis to identify, analyze, and solve quality and other problems in their area.

WHERE DO MEMBERS COME FROM?

Ideally, members of a particular team should be from the same work area, or who do similar work, so that the problems they select will be familiar to all of them.

HOW MANY MEMBERS ARE IN A TEAM?

An ideal size is seven or eight members. The size can vary from a low of three members to a high of about fifteen. The size must never be so great that each and every member cannot have sufficient time to participate and contribute at each meeting.

WHAT ARE SOME OF THE WESTERN WORLD COMPANIES THAT HAVE INSTALLED THIS TYPE OF EMPLOYEE PARTICIPATION PROGRAM?

A partial list includes plants or divisions of the following organizations: J.C. Penney Co., U.S. Naval Ordnance, Uniroyal, Federal Aviation Administration, Ampex, Super Sagless, Armstrong Cork, Firestone, R.J. Reynolds Tobacco, Salt River Project, Bendix Corp., C.T.S., Yazaki — Australia, Hysla — Mexico, Singer-Kearfott, Amerock, Perfex, Victor Business Machines, Visual Graphics, Michigan Bell Telephone, Rolls Royce — England, Volvo — Sweden, Johnson & Johnson — Brazil, and many many others.

WHAT ARE THE OBJECTIVES?

*	Reduce errors and enhance quality
*	Inspire more effective teamwork
*	Promote job involvement
*	Increase employee motivation
*	Create a problem-solving capability
*	Build an attitude of "problem prevention"
*	Improve company communications
*	Develop harmonious manager/worker relationships
*	Promote personal and leadership development
*	Develop a greater safety awareness
*	Promote cost reduction

WHY THE EMPHASIS ON QUALITY?

A higher level of quality will make for happier customers and promote repeat business. Further, reduced levels of defects and scrap are directly translatable into higher productivity and profits -- profits that spell increased job security.

WHAT ORGANIZATIONS CAN USE IT?

Every organization offering goods or services needs to involve its people in a quality consciousness. Every business, every industry and every organization, regardless of its product or purpose can benefit greatly from the participation of all its people. They are now used in such diverse industries as merchandising, hospitals, banking, insurance, and many more.

IS THIS A NEW IDEA?

These teams (called Quality Circles) were conceived in Japan, in 1961, under the leadership of Dr. Kaoru Ishikawa, then an engineering professor at Japan's prestigious Tokyo University. Dr. Ishikawa, under the sponsorship of the Union of Japanse Scientists and Engineers (JUSE), tied together the theories of behavioral scientists such as Maslow, Herzberg, and McGregor, to the quality sciences introduced to Japan by Drs. Deming and Juran. The result was a "system" that was called Quality Control Circles. The first Circles were registered with JUSE during May, 1962.

HOW IS THE PROGRAM ORGANIZED?

A program is an integrated system made up of several parts:

* The members themselves
* The leaders
* The facilitator (program coordinator)
* Steering Committee

HOW MANY TEAMS IN A GIVEN AREA?

In a clerical operation, for example, where 25 individuals do identical jobs, how are the 7 or 8 persons selected? No selection is made. Nor is membership rotated. If all 25 want to be members, then three groups are formed. Remember, the team represents an investment in people and in the organization. Experience shows that the three teams in this instance would not duplicate each other's activities. Each will contribute in its own way and that contribution will benefit the others.

HOW LONG DO MEETINGS NORMALLY LAST AND HOW OFTEN ARE THEY HELD?

As a rule of thumb, meetings occur once a week and each meeting lasts for approximately one hour. However, some companies have introduced variations. An example is a half-hour meeting once a week. Another variation is to hold a one or a two hour meeting every two weeks.

HOW DOES THE PROCESS WORK?

The following diagram graphically depicts the steps involved:

Problem identification results from any of:
*   The members
*   Management
*   Staff or technical experts.
Typically, several problems are identified. Problem selection is a prerogative of the members.

Problem analysis is performed by the members, with assistance, if needed, by the appropriate technical experts.

The members make their recommendation directly to its manager using a powerful communication technique described as "The Management Presentation." This technique is described in greater detail in a later section of this book.

WHAT TAKES PLACE DURING A MEETING?

Any of several activities may occur during a meeting, such as:
* Identifying a theme or problem to work on
* Getting training as required to better enable members to analyze problems
* Analyzing a problem
* Preparing recommendations for implementing a solution
* Participating in a presentation to management.

HOW SHOULD MEMBERS APPROACH PROBLEMS?

Members should approach problems with a positive attitude -- one that says, "We can do it!" There is a tendency to shrug off problems with, "Why bother, management will not listen anyway." The fact is that well in excess of 80% of recommendations are approved by management. Open discussion and brainstorming, with everyone participating in a positive and cooperative manner, will shed new light on any problem.

HOW IMPORTANT IS IT FOR MEMBERS TO ESTABLISH OBJECTIVES AND MILESTONES?

Very important. Members are encouraged to establish an objective and develop a plan to achieve it. The plan is further broken into milestones so that progress can be constantly measured against the plan. In fact, the training includes the use of charting techniques so that progress can be posted and serve as a constant reminder.

WHAT IF A PROJECT OVERLAPS INTO OTHER ORGANIZATIONS?

This should be avoided. Usually, there are plenty of problems in one's own area. However, if an overlap does occur, an effort should be made to work with the employees in the affected area. Also, management of all organizations involved should be kept advised.

HOW DO MEMBERS USE THE SERVICES OF SPECIALISTS?

Although members are largely a "do-it-your-self-er," it is frequently necessary for them to contact the organizations' experts in given fields, such as quality, engineering, safety, maintenance, etc. This communication is strongly encouraged, and the invitations to attend meetings and offer advice and consultation should be made by the facilitator through normal channels. The specialists thus called upon serve as consultants, while the members retain responsibility for solving the problems.

WHAT IS THE STEERING COMMITTEE?

Fundamentally, the Steering Committee must set goals and objectives for the team activities. It establishes operational guidelines and controls the rate of expansion. It should be presided over by a chairman and decisions reached by democratic process -- one man, one vote.

WHO SHOULD BE ON THE STEERING COMMITTEE?

Representatives from major departments within the company should be members of the Steering Committee. The facilitator should be a member also.

WHAT IS A FACILITATOR?

The facilitator is the individual responsible for coordinating and directing team activities within a given organization.

WHO IS THE LEADER?

Experience demonstrates that member activities will have a greater chance of success when the supervisor is the initial leader. The concept gains quicker acceptance when it fits into the existing organizational structure. The supervisor is already designated to perform a leadership role in that structure. If it did not operate within the existing organizational set-up, it might be viewed by some as a competing organization.

CAN ANYONE OTHER THAN THE SUPERVISOR BE THE LEADER?

Of course. It will probably evolve in the following manner. The supervisor becomes the first leader. Later, the leader identifies another individual, usually a lead person to act as an assistant leader.

IS THERE A RELATIONSHIP BETWEEN TEAM ACTIVITIES AND THE JOB?

The members are people who normally work together. The projects they select to work on always relate to the work they do.

WHAT ARE GENERAL PROBLEM AREAS SELECTED BY MEMBERS?

Paperwork, hardware, communications, service and processes are but a few of the general categories of problems worked on by members. Virtually anything which affects the quality of their work is a candidate.

DO MEMBERS EVER RUN OUT OF PROBLEMS?

No. They may occasionally think so, but a brainstorming session usually surfaces many problems that need immediate attention.

IS "PROBLEM PREVENTION" AN APPROPRIATE THEME?

It is most apropriate and should be enthusiastically encouraged. When a team has passed the point of "putting out fires" and starts looking ahead for ways to preventing them, it has achieved a major milestone. This is a form of quality consciousness that insures that quality will be built into the product and not "inspected" in.

ARE SAFETY THEMES ACCEPTABLE?

Absolutely. Most safety themes also have a relationship to quality. But, whether the tie-in is there or not, safety themes should be encouraged.

DON'T SUGGESTIONS GET COSTLY TO IMPLEMENT?

Rarely.   90% of the recommendations either cost nothing or can be financed from normal department budgets.   Remember, members are encouraged to select themes where they are the experts.   Thus, they will likely be the ones that subsequently effect the recommended changes, and they typically do so in a most cost conscious manner.

ATTITUDE RESULTS

Opinion surveys taken among leaders and members consistantly result in unanimous or near unanimous agreement that:

*   Quality has been improved
*   Morale has been enhanced
*   They are cost effective
*   Activities shoulld be continued and
        extended to others

WHAT IS THE MANAGEMENT PRESENTATION?

A management presentation is where the leader and members describe to their manager what project they have been working on and what recommendations they wish to make concerning it.   Participants use charts that they have prepared.   This event represents a most exciting form of participation, communication, and recognition to all.

WHY ARE MANAGEMENT PRESENTATIONS IMPORTANT?

Management presentations promote communication. Managers are personally informed of   activities and accomplishments.   The members gain recognition for their contributions.   Morale is bolstered by this periodic opportunity to deal directly with the manager and to be reassured of support for their activities.

WHEN IS A MANGEMENT PRESENTATION MADE?

A presentation should be made to:

* Show completed projects
* Make recommendations
* Provide status on long term projects

WHAT IS THE RECOMMENDED FREQUENCY OF THE MANAGE-
MENT PRESENTATION?

Approximately every three months.

WHAT TRAINING IS PROVIDED?

Leader training is provided by your facilitator
during a concentrated three day class. The leader
then trains the members (with help as necessary
from the facilitator) during a portion of each
meeting. This member training takes place over a
period of several weeks. Thereafter, additional
training is provided only as required or as a
refresher.

WHEN ARE MEMBERS TRAINED?

During their meetings, which are used both for
training and for the study of projects.

WHAT ARE THE TECHNIQUES?

The most common techniques are:

* Brainstorming
* Data Gathering (Sampling)
* Check Sheets
* Pareto Analysis

*   Cause-&-Effect Problem Analysis
*   Presentation Techniques

NOTES

FIRST MEETING.

Welcome the members and guests.

Introduce the facilitator and any guests, if present.

Answer the question, "What is it?"

State what is <u>not</u> within the charter of members, such as involvement with pay rates, grievances, personnel matters, etc. Point out that there are other channels for dealing with such matters.

Tell what your organization's objectives are for this activity: improved quality, safety, better communication, cost reduction, improvement of competitive position, job security, etc.

Briefly describe the details of how this activity operates. Point out that members will receive training in problem analysis techniques, they will be involved in selecting the problems in their work area that will be taken up as team projects, they will work out the solutions to problems they select for attention, and that they will be directly involved in presenting recommendations to management.

Name various organizations that have installed this type of employee participation activity. Examples are: General Electric, Xerox, Lincoln National Life, Reynolds Tobacco, Uniroyal, Firestone, The Singer Company, F.A.A., U.S. Navy, U.S. Air Force, U.S. Army, Ampex, RCA, Hewlett-Packard, Lockheed, Boeing, Armstrong World Industries, Bendix, Michigan Bell Telephone, Coors, Northrup, Hughes, Martin-Marietta, TRW, J.C. Penney's Catalog Centers, and hundreds of others.

Tell them that Japan initiated the first teams (called Quality Control Circles or QC Circles) in 1962 and that it was not until the mid 1970s that they were first adopted in the Western World.

Let them know that there is an International Association of Quality Circles which was founded in late 1977, for the purpose of furthering the Quality Circle concept world-wide, and they may join, if they wish. It publishes a quarterly magazine which will prove to be of interest to them.

Describe how your organization got started in this activity, explain the role of the steering committee and name its members.

Explain how the facilitator provides support and assistance to the members and others.

If it has not already come from someone in the group, ask the question "What's in it for me?" Some of the answers you can provide include:

* Training in problem analysis.

* The opportunity to identify the problems you have been living with and no one seems to care about.

* Being recognized as the "expert" in your area.

* Being allowed to select the problems to be analyzed.

* Having the chance to actually analyze the selected problem.

* The opportunity to present recommended problem solutions directly to management.

* The chance to contribute to enhancing the organization's quality reputation,

to make it more competitive, and
to assure greater job security.

Distribute the manuals to the members. Call
attention to the questions and answers in the
first chapter. Urge them to remember to ask any
unanswered questions at the next meeting. Also,
point out that there are work sheet problems and
quizzes to aid the learning process and suggest
that they use them.

Introduce the training course. List the subjects
that will be covered: Case Study + Problem
Prevention Techniques, Brainstorming, Data Col-
lecting Techniques, Data Collecting Formats Plus
Graphs, Decision Analysis Using Pareto, Basic
Cause & Effect Problem Analysis, Process C & E
Problem Analysis, and The Management Presentation.

Explain that the A-V modules for those subjects
contain everything that apears in the member
manuals, plus many more illustrations, so the book
should be set aside while the A-Vs are being
presented.

Also, let the members know that it is alright
to interrupt the A-V presentation with pertinent
comments and questions. You will be glad to stop

the A-V equipment at any point they would like you to do so, so that any misunderstandings can be cleared up.

Present the A-V module on Case Study + Problem Prevention Techniques, stopping where suggested in the manual and elsewhere if helpful.

Get maximum involvement in a discussion of the material presented. Be sure to ask for examples of tie-ins between what was presented and what is encountered in actual on-the-job situations.

Urge the members to complete the worksheet exercise.

Ask the members to give some thought to a nickname for their group, if they would like to have one. (Almost all do)

Ask them to make a list of items they would want to include in a Code of Conduct, which they will create at the next meeting.

Give the quiz on Case Study + Problem Prevention Techniques.

Suggest that the chapter on Brainstorming be read

before the next meeting.

Announce the date, time, and place of the next meeting.

Thank the attendees for their attention and cooperation.

While details are still fresh in your mind, write the minutes of this meeting. If practical, have them typed in an organized format, which will serve as a model, prior to the next meeting. This is the only time you will take the minutes. At the beginning of the next meeting you will either get a volunteer or select someone to handle this detail.

Confer with your facilitator if required.

CHAPTER TWO

CASE STUDY & PROBLEM PREVENTION TECHNIQUES

This case study will illustrate how a problem is handled. Just as important, perhaps even more so, it will present techniques of how to prevent problems in the first place.

STOP THE A-V

    Comment: *The Case Study you are about to see will introduce new terminology and techniques to show how they interrelate. Subsequent training sessions will prepare you to be able to use them easily.*

☐ Most organizations have a mailing room on the premises.

Most mail requires only normal handling. Some pieces are classified and need special processing. Certified and registered letters also call for extra attention.

☐ This company's mail room doubles as a shipping department for cartons and crates going to customers.

☐ The supervisor has just completed a leader training course. Also trained in the same class were supervisors from manufacturing and office areas.

☐ He gets his people together to give them information and answer their questions about their upcoming group involvement.

They are introduced to the facilitator who coordinates all groups in the organization. The facilitator will stay in close touch and attend many of their meetings.

☐ One of the important tasks is to have a member maintain the minutes of the meetings.

☐ The leader lists the various training techniques they will be taught.

He explains that the first training session emphasizes problem prevention techniques. The message is clear -- the best way to control problems is to avoid them.

Brainstorming techniques are employed in a number of situations. Everyone gets involved and contributes.

BRAINSTORMING

DATA COLLECTING

Techniques

To solve problems, data must be collected. The leader explains that ways to do this on a sampling basis will be described in one of the classes. Sampling permits it to be done in a way that saves time and effort for members.

Data Collection

FORMATS

Plus

GRAPHS

A variety of forms are available and can be used to ease and speed the collection of data. The design and use of graphs and charts will also be demonstrated.

DECISION ANALYSIS

Using

PARETO

Decision analysis techniques aid members when choices must be made.

Basic Cause & Effect

PROBLEM ANALYSIS

Members do not simply identify problems for others to solve. Cause-&-Effect problem analysis is a favorite technique for them to use.

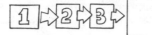

**Process
Cause & Effect**

Problem Analysis

An interesting and specialized variation can be used most effectively to pin point major causes of problems.

Members learn how to communicate their recommendations to management in a most powerful way -- the management presentation.

☐ This introductory session continues until all questions have been answered.

☐ They start meeting on a regular basis wherein the various training techniques are presented.

☐ After they learn the principles of brainstorming they decide to put this new knowledge into practice by having a brainstorming session to identify the various problems they might work on.

Members then review each item and use a special process to identify the key ones. These are circled for quick identification.

These top items are then prioritized using a voting process to achieve group consensus.

☐ The number one item becomes the project for the group to work on. They decide on a course of action to do the analysis. Data is needed. They decide to collect it on a sampling basis to save time and effort. To do so, an action plan is compiled.

☐ The leader arranges for a member of the technical staff to visit their next meeting where he is briefed. Generally he is satisfied, but is able to make a few helpful suggestions. He seems pleased that they are so enthusiastic and urges them to keep him informed so he can assist if they wish.

CHECK SHEET

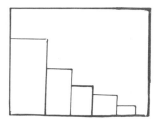

With that encouragement, they design a check sheet and use it to easily collect the data they need.

Decisions have to be made. The data collected on the check sheet is used to construct a Pareto chart that graphically depicts the degree and magnitude of the various alternatives.

The number one priority as portrayed by the Pareto chart becomes the target for a detailed Cause-&-Effect analysis. It is hoped that this will disclose the true cause of the problem. Let us assume the problem is "Incorrect postage on letter."

☐ The Cause-&-Effect problem analysis is led by the leader but involves all of the members in suggesting every possible cause they can think of.

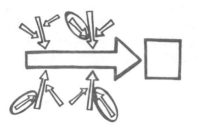

Next, each of these possible causes is examined and discussed to whatever depth desired prior to a vote. The causes gaining the most votes are circled.

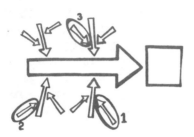

Finally, each of the circled causes is subjected to even further analysis and deliberation and voted on. The priority ranking: #1, #2, #3, etc. is written in as shown.

Verification. How do we verify if the number one most probable cause is the true one? Remember, the problem, was "Incorrect postage on letter." If the number one most likely cause is "Defective postage meter," members would suggest ways to verify it. Then, after selecting a method, they would apply it before proceeding further.

Having verified the true cause, only one task remains -- that of determining the recommended solution. Total involvement is obtained by conducting a brainstorming session to surface a variety of possible solutions.

The all important management presentation is where members recommend their proposed solution to the manager. The manager reviews the recommendation in light of the bigger picture and makes a decision to approve it. This is the first of a series of presentations that occur approximately every two to four months from now on.

☐ The management presentation is used as an opportunity to thank staff specialists who provide assistance in any way to the group.

☐ Initially, members will spend time "putting out fires."

But, the phase that follows is the one that ultimately has the big benefits -- problem prevention.

☐ This group is no different. During subsequent meetings a trend begins to develop -- an increasing emphasis on problem prevention. Their organizational manager is aware of this new direction and voices hearty support.

STOP THE A-V

Comment: *Projects should ideally be taken from the area where members work -- where they are the experts.*

Ask: *In our area, do we have projects or problems that this group could work on?*

Answer: *General discussion.*

PROBLEM PREVENTION

The most advanced teams acquire an intense interest in preventing problems before they occur.

☐ A "stitch in time saves nine" is a familiar phrase.

☐ Problems are avoided by the simple expediency of taking simple precautions that require almost no expenditure of time.

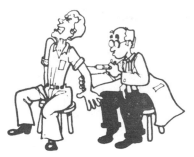

Vaccinations are familiar to most of us as a problem preventative technique.

☐ A coat of paint can go a long way to ward off future problems. This is especially applicable in paint protecting metal surfaces that would otherwise rust and corrode.

☐ Now that the members have begun to pursue the subject of problem prevention, they decided to use a brainstorming session to draw out everyone's ideas. They are convinced that by simply identifying problem prevention techniques and talking about them, fewer problems will occur.

STOP THE A-V

Comment: *You are about to see a number of ways that members use to prevent problems. As you observe each, ask yourselves these questions:*

1. Is this a technique I have used in the past?
2. Are we doing it now?
3. Can we adapt it and use it now?

Training in special skills can add assurance that the job will be done right the first time. This training might be done as simply as one-on-one by the supervisor, or in group sessions.

☐ Detailed work instructions that have been carefully prepared will add assurance and confidence that the work will be correctly done in the first place.

☐ Even greater assurance of compliance occurs when the work instructions are organized as a check list. Thus, steps are not missed, are done in the proper order, and it becomes easier for someone else to pick up where another leaves off.

One member suggests increased use of "workmanship samples." These are completed units that are available for comparison purposes. One might be available to each employee or to a group of employees doing the same thing.

☐ Another suggestion along the same line is the use of a photograph if the actual workmanship sample is not available.

☐ "Buddy checks" will prevent problems from occurring because a fellow employee quickly examines your work before it is passed on.

Members almost always profit from a careful examination of the Job Instructions affecting them. They may update them to reflect the best way to do their jobs.

☐ Each employee shall examine the paperwork and/or parts coming to him to assure that errors are not present. One member adds, "Even better, why not have each person sign-off on completed work before it gets passed on?"

☐ Half the time the person who creates an error won't admit it. Let's work on a system of traceability so that we will all assume responsibility for our work."

Another points out that manufacturing employees are often provided with measuring instruments to check or gauge their own work. "Maybe we can somehow use the same concept here."

☐ A member speaks up, "That would enable an employee to do something called a '1st Article Inspection.' It's done by the individual who has to make or process, say, 50 identical units. He does the first one, examines it carefully for flaws, and proceeds to make copies only when it is crystal clear that it is perfect."

"Sure, good idea," comments another member, "But that means making sure such instruments and gauges get regular calibration checks. Nothing stays calibrated for long."

2-14

☐ There are other techniques to aid in the prevention of problems.

Absenteeism tends to cause an increased error rate. Reduced absenteeism and problem prevention go hand-in-hand. Why? Because the absent employee is usually replaced with someone with less knowhow and experience and with less capability of avoiding errors.

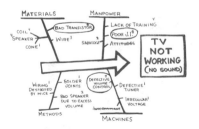

Cause-&-Effect problem analysis indirectly aids in holding down errors. How? The participation by members in identifying possible causes serves to alert members as to potential problem areas. Thus, a new problem prevention awareness is created.

☐ The same benefit can follow if the effect is a good one. Like the coffee surprisingly tastes better than ever. It may seem like a waste of time. But, it is vital that causes of a sudden unexpected good effect be identified so that steps may be taken to make it stay that way.

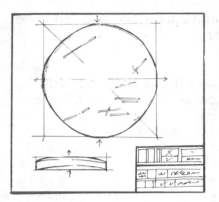

Use drawing to mark the location of defects as they occur. This will provide new knowledge on what and where errors are happening and do so in a most graphic way.

Collecting defect data on a regular check sheet is likewise an excellent method of building an awareness as to the various types and quantities of errors.

☐ This data is collected on a sampling basis whenever possible to minimize the expenditure of time. Often this data is used as the basis for constructing histogams and control charts.

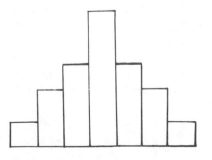

Information from samples become the basis for constructing histograms. These provide important clues that warn of problems.

Data from samples can be used to easily construct X.R Control charts that plot trends that signal when a process is going out of control.

The Np control chart is similar in many respects. It signals the alarm when the process gets too close or exceeds the upper control limit line.

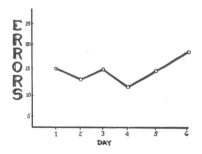

Then, of course, there is the plain and simple line graph -- that is, there are no upper or lower control limit lines. For many applications it is quite adequate to chart progress by this means.

☐   The display of charts in the work area provides the all important feedback to members and other employees that can serve to reinforce their determination to prevent problems.

A most important tactic is to identify key points in the process that would trigger errors if they go out of control. Recognizing this, develop an <u>alternative</u> plan that can snap into action quickly in such an event to dramatically curtail the potential damage.

Communicating gains from practicing the precepts of problem prevention is important because it provides the recognition so essential to maintain and continue the improvement.

WORK SHEET

1. People who work with you will be asking, "What is it and how does it operate?" You will get these and other questions.

    Assignment: In 100 words or less, describe this activity to someone who is unfamiliar with them.

2. Problem prevention is extremely important to assure constant improvement in quality, cost and attitudes.

    Assignment: From the information presented in this section, describe one problem prevention technique you can utilize on your job.

NOTES

QUIZ

1. Who can suggest problems for the team to work on?

   a. Leader
   b. Members
   c. Management
   d. Staff personnel
   e. Any of the above

2. Problem analysis sessions are normally led by:

   a. A member
   b. The Leader
   c. The facilitator
   d. An engineer or staff person whose area of expertise relates to the problem

3. The most common way to identify problems to work on:

   a. One-on-one interviews with each member
   b. Written submittals by members
   c. Brainstorming

4. Problem analysis for the group is primarily the responsibility of:

   a. Leader
   b. Leader and members
   c. Management
   d. Staff personnel
   e. Any of the above

5. Who <u>selects</u> the problem the members will analyze?

   a. Management or technical staff
   b. Steering Commmittee
   c. Facilitator
   d. Leader
   e. Members

6. A decision analysis technique called Pareto identifies the major problem. What technique is then used to locate the cause of that problem?_____

7. The management presentation is sometimes used to merely present status on an on-going project.

   True_____   False_____

8. A line graph and a control chart are similar in what way?_____

   _____

9. Members should not engage in problem prevention techniques until all their obvious problems have been solved.

   True_____   False_____

10. The basic techniques must be significantly modified before being used by office employees?

    True_____   False_____

11. The title usually given to the man or woman providing the overall coordination is_____

    _____

12. Name six problem prevention techniques:

    1._____
    2._____
    3._____
    4._____
    5._____
    6._____

QUIZ ANSWERS

1. Any of the above. This is where they are building the list of problems they <u>could</u> work on. The selection comes later.

2. The leader.

3. Brainstorming. The second most likely waY is as a result of one-on-one interviews with each member. Often, these are conducted by the leader.

4. Leader and members.

5. Members.

6 Cause & Effect Problem Analysis.

7. True. Especially when the project has been underway for some time and is still far from being complete.

8. The central feature of both is the line representing "actuals" as they occur. The control chart differs primarily because of the addition of "outer-limit lines that the "actual" line is expected to remain within.

9. False.

10. False. They are effective in a broad variety of work situations.

11. Facilitator.

12. A variety of answers apply. Among them are:

   * Additional training
   * Use of detailed work instructions
   * Use of "workmanship samples"
   * Use of photographs as a guide

* "Buddy checks"
* Updating of job instructions
* Careful examination of incoming parts and/or paperwork
* Traceability
* Providing gauges to allow employees to check their own work
* "1st article examinations" to assure the first of a series of identical units is perfect before doing the remainder
* Regular calibration of machines and gauges

Other factors contribute to problem prevention. These include:

* Absenteeism reduction
* Drawings showing the location of defects
* Collection of defect data
* Histograms
* Construction of control charts and other charts to provide feedback to group members
* Participation in brainstorming sessions that take up the subject of problem prevention
* Participation in Cause & Effect Problem Analysis sessions. These heighten the awareness of members towards problem prevention.

SECOND MEETING

Welcome the members and guests.

Introduce any guests present.

Ask for - and get - a volunteer to act as the secretary and to keep the minutes of each meeting, per the format you have established.

Have the minutes of the last meeting read and approved.

Review and discuss the material on Case Study + Problem Prevention Techniques; and re-do the quiz if helpful.

Discuss any completed worksheet exercises. Give particular attention to the second item of the exercise.

Introduce Brainstorming, considered to be one of the most enjoyable of all of the team activities.

Present the A-V module, stopping where suggested in the manual and elsewhere if helpful.

Get maximum involvement in a discussion of the

material presented.

Urge the members to complete the worksheet exercise.

Prepare a large sheet of paper with the title, "Code of Conduct" clearly marked on it.

It may help to speed things up if you read the list below of rules that other teams have included in their codes of conduct.

* *Attend all meetings and be on time*

* *Listen to, and show respect for the views of other members*

* *Make others feel a part of the group*

* *Criticize ideas, not persons*

* *Take responsibility to help other members participate more fully*

* *Be open to, and encourage the ideas of others*

* *Every member is responsible for the*

team's progress

*   Maintain a friendly attitude

*   Strive to assure enthusiasm

*   Everyone is equal during meetings

*   Give chance to help others express
    themselves more, even if it means less
    personal participation

*   The only stupid question is the one
    that isn't asked

*   Participate according to the golden
    rule

*   Keep an open mind and look for merit
    in the ideas of others

*   Listen carefully to the ideas and
    contributions of others

*   Pay attention -- avoid disruptive
    behavior

*   Attend meetings regularly and partici-

pate in discussions

* Avoid actions that delay progress

* Carry out assignments on schedule

* Ensure that credit is given to those to whom it is due

* Show thanks and appreciation to non-members who give assistance

* Avoid conflict during meetings

* Avoid criticism and scarcasm toward the ideas of others

* No disruptive side conversations

* Maintain a friendly atmosphere at all times

* Speak up and express ideas

* Always strive for win-win situations

* Don't lecture unless you are an expert

* Don't give solutions -- find causes first

* Don't belittle the ideas or opinions of others -- you are not the judge

* Before you criticize, give praise and honest appreciation

* Ask questions instead of giving orders

* Help others to save face

* Praise every improvement no matter how little

* Use encouragement

Explain the rules of brainstorming, and get a volunteer to write the ideas on the sheet as they are stated. If fifteen or more individuals will be involved, get two persons to do the writing while you "direct traffic." It is important that everyone involved can see what's written on the sheet.

Brainstorm, per the instructions in the manual.

When the flow of ideas stops, make a clear-cut transition to the evaluation stage.

At the appropriate point, get the members to vote for as many ideas as they feel are important. Subsequent voting may require a refined system. For example, if the brainstorming group is small and the number of circled ideas is large, have the members vote for as many as they wish. But, if the group is large and the number of ideas is small, you might limit the number each can vote for. This is a matter of judgment.

When the votes are tallied, the items to be considered for inclusion in the Code of Conduct are written in the decending order of importance. Then, a vote can be taken to determine how many of them to include in the final draft. (Usually a code contains eight or ten items)

Have the Code of Conduct written or printed large enough so that members can read it from their seats, and post it before each meeting.

If there is sufficient time to do it, brainstorm a name for the group. If not, tell the members it will be done at the next meeting.

Ask the members to begin thinking about what problems in the work area the they might undertake to resolve.

Give the quiz on brainstorming.

Suggest that the chapter on Data Collecting Techniques be read before the next meeting.

Announce the date, time, and place of the next meeting.

Thank attendees for their attention and cooperation.

Make sure the secretary prepares the minutes.

Confer with your facilitator, if required.

MINUTES

Name	Organization	Leader's Name

Attendees:

_____ _____ _____
_____ _____ _____
_____ _____ _____
_____ _____ _____

Minutes:

Action Items:

Recorder's Name	Date

CHAPTER THREE

BRAINSTORMING

Brainstorming, explained in its most basic way, is using a group of people to stimulate the production of ideas.

☐ It is almost always more effective than trying to generate ideas alone.

☐ The effectiveness of brainstorming in unlocking the creative power of the group has long been recognized.

☐ Prior to starting it is vital to identify what topic will be brainstormed. In this instance the members are being asked to determine what problems exist in their work area.

☐ However, it is important to be as precise as possible in stating the topic to be brain-stormed. Stating, "PROBLEMMS WITHIN OUR WORK AREA," is a decided improvement over simply stating it as "PROBLEMS." That was much too general.

This represents an even further improvement in stating the topic clearly and precisely.

☐ Brainstorming works best when certain guide-lines or rules are followed. The leader will review these prior to each session.

Each member, in rotation, is asked for ideas. This continues until all ideas have been exhausted.

☐ Each member offers only <u>one</u> idea per turn, regardless of how many he or she has in mind.

☐ Strive for quantity of ideas to maximize the effectiveness of the team process.

Not everyone has an idea during each rotation. When this occurs, just say, "Pass."

☐ No idea should be treated as stupid. To criticize or belittle someone is to surely curtail the creativeness of team members.

For some it will be their first attempt to speak out during a brainstorming session. It may take courage to start. Be patient. Welcome and encourage their ideas. Their enthusiastic support is essential.

☐ Good natured laughter and informality should be encouraged to enhance the climate for innovative activity. Obviously, on the other hand, derisive laughter will have an unwelcome and dampening effect.

Exaggeration should be encouraged. It may add humor and it certainly adds a creative stimulus to the process.

☐ After the rules have been explained, the brainstorming session commences.

☐ The leader will often have to abreviate a lengthy idea into a few words. That's fine, but the originator must agree.

During brainstorming, no evaluation of suggested ideas should occur. This applies equally to the leader. Not just a negative comment but even something like, "Hey, that's good!" No comments, please.

☐ The process will be speeded if a member writes the ideas as they are given.

STOP THE A-V

>   *Ask:*   *Why is there so much importance placed on preventing any kind of evaluation during the brainstorming process?*

>   *Answers:*   1.   *To avoid dampening the creative spirit of the group.*
>   2.   *To maximize the quantity of ideas received.*

Finally, the brainstorming has been completed when all ideas have been exhausted. This massive number of ideas must be critically examined and narrowed down.

☐ In the interest of time, a simple voting technique is used. It works because the members are the experts in their area. Members vote on each idea. The leader records each vote next to the idea. Members can vote for as many ideas as they feel have value. Only supporting votes are taken. No one is asked to vote against an idea.

Draw a circle around those ideas that received the most votes. The members decide how many of the top ideas will be so identified.

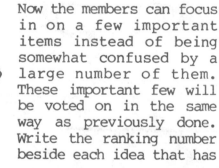

Now the members can focus in on a few important items instead of being somewhat confused by a large number of them. These important few will be voted on in the same way as previously done. Write the ranking number beside each idea that has been circled.

STOP THE A-V

Ask: *Why is the voting process used?*

Answers: 1.   *It is fast*
         2.   *Everyone participates*
         3.   *There is provision for discussing the pros and cons (if desired) prior to each vote.*

☐ What about discussion? A member can halt the voting on any idea and argue for or against it. Others can join in if they wish. Only when the discussion has subsided will the vote take place.

☐ What are examples of topics for brainstorming?

A Code of Conduct represents the rules by which members want to play. This is a favorite topic, particularly for a new team.

☐ New teams often adopt a nickname. The variety is endless and includes, for example, "The Seekers," "The James Bonders," and "The Investigators."

☐ Some new groups have used brainstorming to identify the objectives they wish to pursue.

☐ Problems and impediments that impair quality, cost, and schedule are excellent subjects for brainstorming. Some will become candidates for future projects.

Identify problems within your own area of expertise and control. Every team has a long list of such problems. Only after these have been resolved should you consider the possibility of working with that "other" group.

Potential problem analysis can be a most productive activity. Brainstorming will help clarify these potential difficulties.

☐ After a problem cause has been identified, members might join in brainstorming for possible solutions.

There are a number of items to keep in mind as you explore the subject of brainstorming.

☐ An agenda distributed prior to the meeting will give members a chance to think about the upcoming brainstorming topic and perhaps have several ideas all set to go when the meeting starts.

Use a large sheet of paper when brainstorming. Everyone can read it and it becomes a permanent record that can be later used in a management presentation.

☐ Overhead projectors, when available, are an excellent substitute for the large sheets of paper. The transparent sheets are easily stored and can also be used in a management presentation.

☐ Blackboards can be seen by everyone but they get erased!

☐ A note pad cannot be seen by everyone and is not suitable for later use in a management presentation.

Look to nature for creative break throughs.

☐ New ideas will be generated by thinking big. Small aircraft spawned visions of huge airliners in the same way that small ships preceded the mammouth ones that followed.

Combinations of existing concepts or units may lead to new and exciting creations. Such was the case when the steam engine and the paddle were combined to power early ships.

☐ A shot of fantasy can aid in shedding the bonds that prevent us from doing creative thinking. An example is to imagine that the laws of gravity can be cancelled.

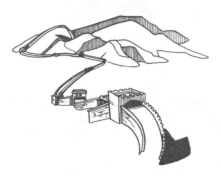

Or, if you are brain-storming for solutions, fantasize that money is absolutely no obstacle. Perhaps something like that happened when the great wall of China was conceived.

☐ Put yourself in the other "person's" place. For instance, a group imagines they are germs in an attempt to figure how they could break through to cause decay!

The pursuit of minification concepts during brainstorming may lead to new and sometimes superior products that often cost less.

☐ Leave the brainstorming record posted when possible. It will likely receive a lot of attention and may have ideas added to it by members and others.

Incubation often occurs after the initial brainstorming session. "Let's sleep on it," is a frequently voiced comment. Later, many innovative ideas may emerge.

☐ The ideas will begin to flow when you ask yourself questions based upon the "Five W's and H: What, Why, When, Where, Who, and How."

☐ Members and others should feel free to add to the brainstorming chart.

☐ If visitors drop in during a brainstorming session, you may decide to invite them to join in. If so, take a minute to explain the rules to avoid possible confusion and embarrassment.

A member occasionally may lead the brainstorming activity.

☐ Finally, get in the habit of identifying, on the brainstorming sheet, who was involved and when it happened. Such information is vital if the analysis is to have any historical value.

WORK SHEET

1. You are the group leader. You are about to conduct a brainstorming session. Several steps must be taken prior to, during, and after brainstorming. These include (not necessarily in the correct order):

    *   The actual brainstorming session
    *   Precisely stating the topic to be brainstormed
    *   Discussion (pro and con) of ideas
    *   Stating the rules
    *   Voting

    Assignment: Rearrange these steps in the order they will occur. Add at least one sentence of explanation to each.

2. You want your members to establish a Code of Conduct. You tell them ahead of time so they can think about it. But, as their leader, you must also do so.

    Assignment: List at least four ideas you will be able to contribute when the session takes place.

3.   Brainstorming techniques are as applicable with members of your family, club and church members, as they are with the people you work with.

Assignment: Conduct a brainstorming session on your own with you preferrably as the leader. In the space below briefly describe it and how well you felt about it.

QUIZ

1. In actual practice, it is unnecessary to repeat the rules of brainstorming prior to every session.

    True_____   False_____

2. It is not essential to write down every idea that is suggested because many are obviously unrelated to the brainstorming topic.

    True_____   False_____

3. A member can suggest more than one idea (e.g. two ideas) per turn when they are closely related.

    True_____   False_____

4. Members must take turns in rotation around the table in suggesting ideas.

    True_____   False_____

5. Laughter of any sort should be avoided during brainstorming.

    True_____   False_____

6. If an idea is offered that another member strongly disagrees with, the session should be halted briefly to discuss why.

    True_____   False_____

7. If the team size is excessively large, (e.g. 18 members), it is then permissable to select a limited number of brainstorming participants to keep things moving fast.

    True_____   False_____

8. Brainstorming is used only to select new themes for the group to pursue.

    True_____   False_____

9. It is best to write ideas on:

    a.   A note pad
    b.   Large sheet of paper
    c.   Blackboard

10. The person writing down the brainstorming ideas is always entitled to take a turn.

    True_____   False_____

11. Normally, non-members at the meeting should be invited to take part in the brainstorming session.

    True_____   False_____

12. When a member says, "Pass," he gives up his chance to take part from that point on.

    True_____   False_____

13. Name several situations where the brainstorming technique can be used:

    1._____

    2._____

    3._____

    4._____

QUIZ ANSWERS

1. False. It takes only a moment to repeat the rules of brainstorming and serves as a needed reminded.

2. False. There should be no criticism of ideas during brainstorming. The unimportant ideas will drop out during voting.

3. False

4. True

5. False. <u>Good</u> <u>natured</u> laughter can be a spur to creative thinking.

6. False

7. False. It would be preferrable to divide into two groups. If this cannot be easily accomplished, then ask if one or two members will help out the leader by writing down ideas as they are called out.

8. False

9. A large sheet of paper. Not only can everyone easily read it but it provides a permanent record.

10. True.

11. True.

12. False.

13.   a.   *Choosing a team name.*

        b.   *Developing a Code of Conduct.*

        c.   *Identifying possible projects.*

        d.   *Identifying various ways to verify if a cause is the true cause.*

        e.   *Identifying a variety of ways a solution could be implemented.*

        f.   *Identifying ways to collect data.*

THIRD MEETING

Welcome the members and guests.

Introduce any guests present.

Have the minutes of the last meeting read and approved.

Review and discuss the material in Brainstorming; and re-do the quiz if helpful.

Discuss any completed worksheet exercises.

Introduce Data Collecting Techniques. Explain that if they are to solve problems, they must have data. This training session will emphasize how to get the necessary information with the minimum expenditure of time and effort. Frequently, this involves some kind of sampling technique. While there are many benefits to sampling, there are also risks.

Present the A-V module - stopping where suggested in the manual and elsewhere if helpful.

Get maximum involvement in a discussion of the material presented.

Urge the members to complete the worksheet exercise.

If a name was not selected for the team at the last meeting you might do it now -- after reviewing the rules of brainstorming.

Begin the process of selecting a problem to work on. Again, review the rules before every brainstorming session whenever guests are present, and when no one but members are present, do so until everyone consistently follows them as a matter of course. You are asking the members to identify those problems they consider to be obstacles or impediments to achieving the highest possible quality and the lowest possible costs. Brainstorming is the technique to maximize the effectiveness of this exercise. Get everybody involved! Be sure they understand that the maximum number of suggestions are needed at this time and that they will later pick the number one problem they wish to adopt as an official team project.

Give assignments to members. Get maximum involvement. Don't volunteer to do anything yourself that someone else can do.

Ask the members to be thinking about the next phase of the current project.

Give the quiz on Data Collecting Techniques.

Suggest that the chapter on Data Collection Formats Plus Graphs be read before the next meeting.

Announce the date, time, and place of the next meeting.

Thank attendees for their attention and cooperation.

Make sure the secretary prepares the minutes.

Confer with your facilitator, if required.

©1980 QUALITY CIRCLE INSTITUTE
Red Bluff, CA., U.S.A.

REPRODUCTION EXPRESSLY
PROHIBITED

MEMBER ATTENDANCE LOG

Name __Scrap Stoppers__   Leader __Jim Smith__   Dep't. __SHP6 A-3__

V – Vacation   P – Present
L – Leave   A – Absent

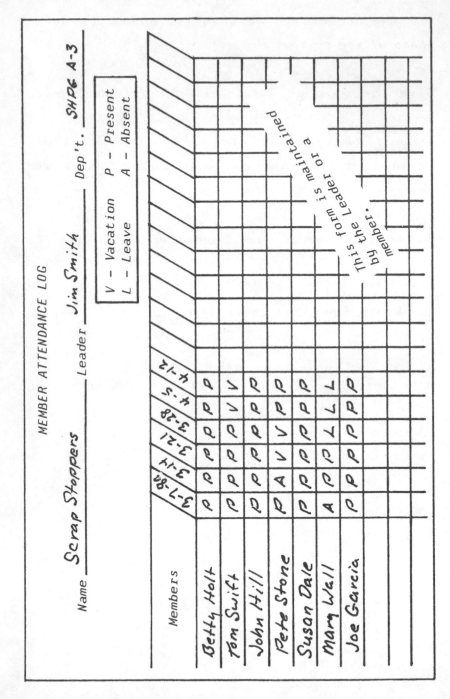

This form is maintained by the Leader or a member.

Members	3-7-84	3-14	3-21	3-28	4-5	4-12
Betty Holt	P	P	P	P	P	P
Tom Swift	P	P	P	V	V	V
John Hill	P	P	P	P	P	P
Pete Stone	P	P	V	V	P	P
Susan Dale	P	P	P	P	P	P
Mary Wall	A	P	L	L	L	L
Joe Garcia	P	P	P	P	P	

CHAPTER FOUR

DATA COLLECTING TECHNIQUES

DATA COLLECTING

TECHNIQUES

If we are to solve problems, and, just as important, prevent others from occuring, we <u>must</u> have information. In this section we will learn how sampling techniques will assist us in the collection of the data we need.

☐ Why sampling? One very important reason is that it saves times.

☐ When we save time, we are automatically also saving money.

Why do we want to collect data? There are two basic purposes:
(1)   Problem analysis
(2)   Problem prevention

☐   To analyze a problem, we must first collect information.   Then, we are in a position to successfully solve it.

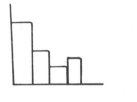

Pareto charts and Cause-&-Effect diagrams are two of the major tools used in problem analysis.

☐   Problem prevention is the other very important purpose of collecting data.

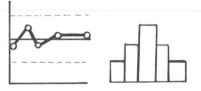

Control charts and histograms are examples of two methods to help prevent problems by keeping the process under control.   Data is required to construct either -- data that can usually be collected in a sampling format.

A 100% examination is not always the most accurate. Fatigue can reduce a person's attention to detail.

☐ Further, there are numerous examples where sampling has produced more accurate results. It is less costly. It requires less time and it may afford the chance to do a more thorough and careful examination of the sample.

The sample (n) can be expected to accurately represent the barrel of wine (N).

☐ Television program ratings are based on minute and carefully selected samples.

Pollsters use tiny samples to determine public opinion. It can be quick, relatively inexpensive, and remarkably accurate.

☐ As little as one drop of your blood is all that's needed to gain all sorts of accurate information about your total blood supply.

☐ Samples are used to test the smog levels of our cities.

☐ Trying to examine 100% of anything can be an exhausting experience; and, as we have pointed out, possibly unnecessary.

☐ 100% would mean examining everything. Rejects would likely be sorted by type of defect.

☐ In the instance of a poll taken on 100% of the city's population to find out who the people want as mayor, it requires that the data be sorted by candidate and counted.

Let's see how sampling can save us time and money in collecting information. How about the question, "How many boys in our community play soccer?" Sampling should be quite adequate.

☐ What percentage of the population has gone ocean surfing? Again, sampling would be the obvious way to get this information.

☐ Some products are destroyed in the process of examining and testing them. Sampling minimizes this loss.

An expensive form of destruct testing is when specialized types of information must be collected. Obviously, sampling is the only way to do it.

☐ There are six steps we should follow in sampling.

1. LEARN THE FACTS

Step 1. Learn the facts. Let's say you are a pollster and want to forecast who is going to be elected mayor of the city. Some things you must learn include: What groups, ethnic and otherwise, make up the city's population? Relative size of each? Average age? Employment statistics of each group? Income levels? Past voting trends? Educational level, etc.

Step 2. Learn how large the lot size is. This is also called the "population" and is abbreviated with the letter capital "N". In the case of the pollster, "N" is the total number of people eligible to vote.

Step 3. A sampling table will tell you how large the sample should be to achieve the degree of accuracy you want. Staff personnel skilled in these techniques can be helpful at this time. An excessive sample size would be a waste of money.

☐ The larger the sample size, the greater the probability of accuracy. In coin tosses, you should get 50% heads and 50% tails, but only 10 tosses could easily result in something like 7 heads and 3 tails. One thousand tosses would be very close to the true odds of 500 each.

STOP THE A-V

Ask: Why might it be wise to call in an expert at this time?

Answers:
1. It may save time.
2. It adds credibility to the analysis.
3. It may be a new learning experience.

Step 4. Select the sample. In our example the pollster decides what voters would form a representative sample. The sample selected would contain voters from all socio-economic levels. In other words, to avoid biasing the results, it would be a "stratified" sample.

Step 5. Each person in the sample group is asked carefully choosen questions.

Step 6. A prediction is made based on the results of the sample. We use the word "prediction" because we cannot be absolutely certain that the sample accurately reflects the condition of the entire lot.

☐ Remember, although sampling can save us time and effort in the process of our collecting the data we need to solve problems, care must be exercised or the results of the sampling may mislead us.

This is an example of bias. The sample comes from one portion of the lot instead of being randomly selected.

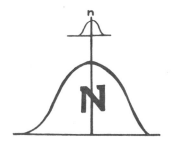

The likelihood of bias is dramatically reduced when the sample is drawn at random from all portions of the lot.

☐   Accessibility is needed to better assure random sampling and no bias. There is a right way and a wrong way to do this.

These two frequency distribution curves illustrate an example of no bias. The sample, small (n), has been well choosen. It is exactly representative of the lot, large (N). Even better, they are exactly on target. This means the lot meets specifications.

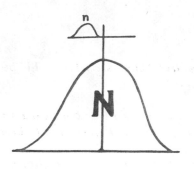

This sample has been poorly selected and is biased. It is not representative of the lot. Unfortunately, based on the sample, the lot will be rejected.

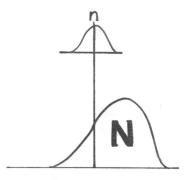

This sample is also poorly selected because it has bias. The lot should fail. But, because the sample passes, the lot will too.

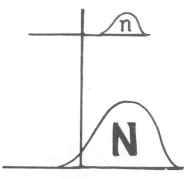

Now for a quiz: (1) Is bias present? No, the sample is exactly representative of the lot. (2) Will the lot pass? No, it does not meet specifications. The sample has done its work well.

> *Ask:* What helps assure the sample will be properly chosen?
>
> *Answers:* 1. There should be equal access to all parts of the lot.
>   2. The lot should be homo-genous.
>   3. The sample size should be sufficiently large.
>   4. The sample should be randomly selected.
>
> *Comment:* The above conditions prevail in a carefully conducted political poll.

☐ In general, there are three common methods of selecting samples.

☐ Random selection means drawing samples from every part of the lot. Two rules apply: (1) Each unit must have an equal opportunity of being selected, and (2) Each unit picked must be completely independent of any other unit.

Systematic selection uses a planned method of picking units. For instance, every fifth unit will be selected. This method is suitable only when it is impossible for external forces to bias the characteristics of the selected units.

Stratification. Pollsters must assure they are taking stratified samples because of the very small sample sizes they depend on. Small samples save money but are potentially very dangerous. Great care must be exercised to select the correct proportion of individuals from every occupation group with additional responsiveness to age, income, education, etc.

☐ Let us take a brief look at ways the members use the information they have collected.

A convenient format to record the data you have collected is in some form of check sheet. It speeds the collection process and makes the data more readily adaptable to comparison and analysis.

Decision analysis techniques depend on first collecting information. Then, it is possible to construct the Pareto chart.

Information must be collected to post charts such as line graphs.

Histograms are often used to measure the uniformity of processes in both production and office areas.

☐ On-going control of a process is superbly maintained with a special type of line graph called an $\overline{X} \cdot R$ Control Chart.

Another kind of control chart is displayed in this illustration.

☐ Your presentation to management will tell the story most convincingly when it is based on a foundation of carefully collected data.

WORK SHEET

1. People in varied occupations collect information using the minimum amount of time and effort possible.

    <u>Assignment:</u> Give an example of using samples for each of the following: (e.g. Doctors take tiny pieces of human tissues for examination in the laboratory).

    Medical (do not use the above example):
    Agriculture:
    Military:
    Factory:
    Office:

2.   You are a pollster. You want to accurately
      determine what percentage of the population
      favors nuclear power and the percentage that
      oppose it. You are determined not to end up
      with biased results.

      Assignment: List at least two errors that
      could cause bias.

3.   It is not always wise to rely on sampling.
      That is, on somethings we want to collect
      information on 100% of the lot.

      Assignment: List those products or pro-
      cesses that you feel are inappropriate
      candidates for sampling.

QUIZ

1. Reasons for gathering data include, (a) to analyze problems, and, (b) to control the process.

   True_____   False_____

2. A random sample helps to assure it will be representative of the lot.

   True_____   False_____

3. The data you need may already be available. Give one example of an individual or an organization that might be able to assist you.

   _____
   _____
   _____

4. Describe any example that illustrates how a sample may be biased.

   _____
   _____
   _____

5. Which term generally described the following? A sample whose average value is different from the average value of the lot.

   a. Bias
   b. Dispersion
   c. Standard deviation

6. An unintentional bias decreases the likelihood the sample will fall within specification.

   True_____   False_____

7. Which of the following depend on first gathering data?

   a. Control Charts
   b. Histograms
   c. Pareto charts
   d. All of them

8. Gathering data using samples collected at pre-determined intervals is referred to as:

   a. Random sampling
   b. Systematic sampling
   c. Stratified sampling
   d. None of the above

9. As a general rule, the size of the sample can be reduced as the size of the lot increases.

   True_____   False_____

10. The foremost reason for employing sampling is that it saves time, money, and effort.

    True_____   False_____

11. Destruct testing is a form of sampling. Give an example.

    _____
    _____
    _____

12. Random sampling can be best assured by:

    a. Simply remembering to include an equal number of units from all portions of the lot
    b. Random tables
    c. Selecting a sample at predetermined intervals, (e.g., every 30 minutes)

QUIZ ANSWERS

1.   *True*

2.   *True*

3.   *Any staff organization. In a clerical organization, you might be aided by accounting or personnel. In manufacturing, it might be quality assurance department or engineering. In actual practice, any number of information sources might be appropriate.*

4.   *Any applicable example is acceptable.*

5.   *Bias*

6.   *True*

7.   *All of them*

8.   *Systematic*

9.   *False*

10. *True*

11. *Any applicable example is acceptable*

12. *Random tables*

NOTES

FOURTH MEETING

Welcome the members and guests.

Introduce any guests present.

Have the minutes of the last meeting read and approved.

Review and discuss the material on Data Collecting Techniques; and re-do the quiz if helpful.

Discuss any completed worksheet exercises.

Introduce Data Collection Formats Plus Graphs. Another way to save time and effort in collecting the data needed to analyze problems is to utilize time-proven formats. These include check lists, drawings showing the location of defects, and check sheets. Information collected is often used to build graphs of various types that will aid in the analysis and also serve double duty as charts in the management presentation.

Present the A-V module, stopping where suggested in the manual and elsewhere if helpful.

Get maximum involvement in a discussion of the

material presented. Ask each member to give an example of a check sheet, check list, or drawing showing the location of a defect found in the area where they work.

Caution members that before undertaking to collect data they should ask Quality Control, Engineering, Accounting, and maybe other departments, if the data already exists.

When collecting data, tend to over collect rather than under collect. It is simpler to eliminate some excessive data than to be frustrated by a later discovery that still more must be collected.

Examples of check sheets include: job applications, quizzes, business forms, check lists for conferences and other functions, bowling score cards, aircraft pre-takeoff lists, kit building instructions, etc.

Urge the members to complete the worksheet exercise.

Continue the process of selecting a team project. If the Brainstorming phase was completed at the last meeting, move on to the next step -- selecting the number one project. Use the voting process described in the Brainstorming training module.

Caution members on two points: 1. Select a problem *entirely* *under* *their* *own* *jurisdiction* *and* *control*. The first project will go more smoothly as a result. 2. Try to *select* *something* *that* *is* *easy* *enough* *for* *the* *team* *to* *complete* *within* *a* *relatively* *short* *period* *of* *time*, rather than have a long drawn out theme that can demoralize and sap the enthusiasm of the group.

Remember to give assignments to members if practical. Get everyone involved!

Ask members to be thinking about the next phase of the project.

Give the quiz on Data Collection Formats Plus Graphs.

Suggest that the chapter on Decision Analysis Using Pareto be read before the next meeting.

Announce the date, time, and place of the next meeting.

Thank the attendees for their attention and

cooperation.

Make sure the secretary prepares the minutes.

Confer with your facilitator, if necessary, concerning setting up a schedule for carrying out the selected project.

CHAPTER FIVE

DATA COLLECTION FORMATS PLUS GRAPHS

The purpose of this section is two-fold. First, "Data Collection Formats." These are the forms members construct to save time in collecting the data they need. The second section is an introduction into the construction and use of various kinds of graphs and charts.

☐ Members need data if they are to solve problems. The use of techniques that speed and simplify this process are welcome. A variety of data collection formats, designed by members, will help accomplish this goal.

WAYS TO COLLECT DATA

1. Check List
2. Drawings
3. Check Sheet

We will study three approaches that enable us to shorten the time it takes to collect the data we need to solve problems: (1) Check lists, (2) Drawings showing the locations of defects (3) Check sheets.

Let us review each way. First, a common example of a check list is the grocery list we are all familiar with.

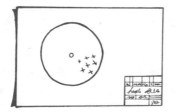

The second type is the drawing that is used to show the location of defects, such as on this record.

CHECK SHEET

ERROR	JUNE 1	JUNE 2	JUNE 3	JUNE 4	TOTAL
ADDITION	ЖHT	ЖHT ////	ЖHT /	ЖHT //	27
MULTI-PLICATION	ЖH ЖH ЖH ////	ЖH ЖH ЖH ЖH ///	ЖH ЖH //// ЖH	ЖH ЖH ЖH	70
OMMISSION	///	ЖHT /	//	/	12
ROUTING	//		/	///	6
TYPING	ЖHT /	ЖHT	ЖHT /	ЖHT //	25
TOTAL	35	42	30	33	140

The third way is with the use of check sheets. They are equally applicable in the office or the factory.

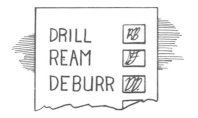

Now we will look at several examples of check lists.

☐ As mentioned, the grocery list is a very familiar type of check list.

DRILL ☑
REAM ☑
DEBURR ☑

A work order assures that each step will be completed and in the correct sequence.

☐   Before a newly designed airplane is flown, a lengthy check list is used to assure that all systems are in proper working condition.

☐   The family that uses a check list will forget fewer items that are essential to a successful vacation trip.

<u>STOP THE A-V</u>

<u>Ask:</u>   Ask for examples of check lists used by members in the performance of their duties. Accept examples from non-job related activities.

Drawings can be used to record the exact location of defects.

☐   One example is an engineering drawing of a music record disk. The location of scratches is indicated right on the drawing.

☐ A company manufacturing face masks for hockey goal keepers painted its mask to show the locations where stitches would have occurred if a well known player had not been protected. Sales went up sharply.

☐ And it doesn't always have to be defects. A large marketing organization sticks flag pins in a map to graphically depict where its sales offices are located.

☐ Athletic teams use this statistical approach in analyzing player effectiveness. Player Number 3 was observed to shoot from one of two general locations. The number "3" was written at the spot he took each shot. If he scored, it was circled. A quick look at the result convinced the player to henceforth avoid trying to shoot while in close to the basket.

☐ Aerial photos are frequently the basis for marketing surveys to determine where shopping centers should be located.

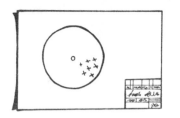

Back to defects. "X's" show the location of scratches on record disks. This is the result of one day's production.

☐ Instead of "X's" you could draw the actual scratch shapes and locations on the drawing.

☐ Symbols can be used when more than one kind of defect is present. The X's represent scratches and the squares show the location of pits in the disk.

☐ The communication process during the management presentation is heightened by the inclusion of drawings that show the locations of defects.

<u>STOP THE A-V</u>

> <u>*Ask:*</u>   *Ask for examples used by members either on or off the job.*

Check Sheets are another popular technique for collecting data. Several steps should be followed:

☐ First, determine the time period when data should be collected. It may take only a few hours or it might require days or possibly months.

☐ Second, decide what variety of information must be collected. It is usually a good idea to collect more than you think necessary. This <u>may</u> result in subtantial future savings in time if the added data is later deemed important.

Third, design a form that will allow you to collect the data you need.

☐ Fourth, record the data on the check sheet you have just designed.

☐ Where does the data come from? In an office it might be found by examining records.

☐ In the factory, the examination of several rejection tags might supply the necessary information for your check sheet.

☐ So, a check sheet is as useful in the office as the factory. But, why collect data? The answer is, "To provide the information we need to analyze problems." Sometimes this also means using the data to build graphs.

☐ One example is a line graph.

☐ Another might be a histogram.

☐ Still another could be a Pareto chart. These are just a few of many possible examples.

If a considerable variety of information is to be recorded on one check sheet, it is possible to do so by using symbols. This contains the identical information as a check sheet you have already seen. Let's take another look.

JUNE			
1	2	3	4

LEGEND

X	ADDITION
I	MULTIPLICATION
△	OMISSION
☐	ROUTING
○	TYPING

CHECK SHEET

ERROR	JUNE				TOTAL
	1	2	3	4	
ADDITION	ЖЖ	ЖЖ IIII	ЖЖ I	ЖЖ II	27
MULTI-PLICATION	ЖЖ ЖЖ ЖЖ IIII	ЖЖ ЖЖ ЖЖ III	ЖЖ ЖЖ III	ЖЖ ЖЖ ЖЖ	70
OMISSION	III	ЖЖ I	II	I	12
ROUTING	II		I	III	6
TYPING	ЖЖ I	ЖЖ	ЖЖ I	ЖЖ II	25
TOTAL	35	42	30	33	140

True, this requires more space than the one using symbols, but it is generally easier and less confusing to use. Use symbols when a large amount of varied data is being gathered.

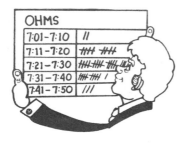

A specialized type of check sheet allows you to collect information that can easily be used to construct a histogram. Use it when repeating the same measurement on identical units. Notice how this check sheet already has taken on the appearance of a histogram.

☐   This becomes even more apparent if you imagine a dotted line running along the perimeter of the tick marks.

☐ A final suggestion. Before designing a check sheet and spending time collecting data, ask the appropriate staff personnel for their advice. They may tell you the information has already been collected.

STOP THE A-V

Ask: *Request examples used by members, either on or off the job.*

☐ Data collection can be an imaginative process. Here are some examples:

If you are lucky, the computer may be able to serve as a fast and reliable way to gather check sheet information.

Memory hooks can be fun as well as useful. This is an example of using a key word in which each letter helps to remind one of an essential task.

☐ The term, "4 Ms", reminds us of four major headings commonly used in Cause-&-Effect Problem Analysis.

☐ Still another memory hook is the "5 Ws and an H."

☐ Another approach that does not really fit any of the above is often referred to as "nemonic." The rings of color on a resister form a code that describe its vital characteristics.

☐ Use the check lists, drawings, and check sheets you have prepared as part of your presentation to management.

STOP THE A-V

Comment: *Explain that they have seen various ways to collect data. The next section of this A-V module will describe how that information can be used to construct charts and graphs.*

Whenever possible, convert the information you have collected into a graph.

☐ It has been said that a picture is worth a thousand words. There is little argument that they save time in the communication process and help the audience to stay alert. Excellent for use in a management presentation.

☐ Column or bar graphs are a favorite way to present data.

The Pareto Chart graphically prioritizes information for decision analysis purposes.

The histogram can be the result if the same measurement is taken on many identical units.

The pie chart clearly depicts the factory output of three competitors.

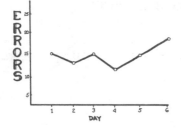

The line graph is frequently employed to visually represent data.

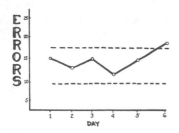

This is the same line graph with control limit lines added. Anytime the line breaks out beyond a control limit it can indicate a problem exists.

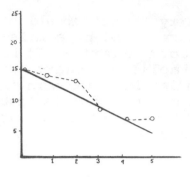

Establishing a target or plan can be done by drawing in a heavy solid line. The actual results are posted with the dotted line as they occur.

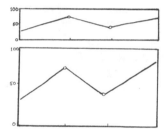

Be careful not to mislead. Although these graphs do not appear to be similar, they actually display the identical information.

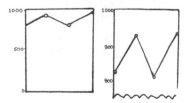

Here's another example of how graphs can mislead. Again, identical information is portrayed, but the impression on the viewer may be completely different.

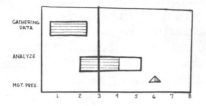

Every project should be accompanied by a milestone chart. This simplified chart is filled in as the work is done, and indicates that the work is ahead of schedule.

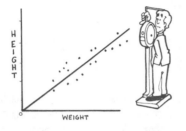

The scatter diagram displays the relationship between two kinds of data. Each plot point represents the height and weight of one man. When a number of people are thus posted the scatter diagram takes on this appearance. A pattern is formed. The shape of that pattern provides clues that assist in understanding the results.

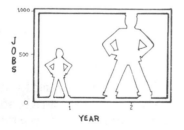

Pictographs are simply graphs that employ pictures to add visual punch to a chart. Avoid this format because, without explanation, it may lead the viewer to believe that the number of jobs increased fourfold when actually it only doubled.

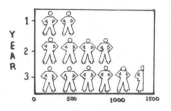

The same information can be conveyed without danger of misinforming if this format is used. The use of a partial symbol is demonstrated during the third year.

☐ Get in the habit of identifying who was involved and when it happened. Such information is vital if the analysis is to have any historical value.

☐ Let's briefly review what we have learned.

☐ Members need data if they are to solve problems. A variety of data collection techniques will help to speed and simplify the process.

WAYS to COLLECT DATA
1. Check List
2. Drawings
3. Check Sheet

Basically, these techniques include: (1) Check lists, (2) Drawings showing the location of defects, and, (3) Check sheets

☐ Whenever you can, present the information you have collected on a graph.

Graphs can communicate your recommendations to management convincingly and with minimum expenditure of time.

WORK SHEET

1. Errors are occuring at an increasing rate in the company mailroom. This is apparent because of a recent rash of complaints. You are not sure of specifics so you decide to do an analysis.

   Facts: On Monday, four letters lacked complete addresses, seven omitted the senders name and address, two had incomplete postage, and five were not processed.

   On Tuesday, two letters lacked complete addresses, six omitted the senders name and address, and eight were not processed.

   On Wednesday, nine omitted the senders name and address, and thirteen were not processed.

   On Thursday, three lacked complete addresses, four omitted the senders name and address, seventeen were torn by the postage metering machine, three had insufficient postage, and two were not processed.

   On Friday, three omitted the senders name and address, five were torn by the postage metering machine, and eleven were delivered to the wrong office within the company.

   Assignment:

   1. Make a check sheet and post the above information to it.
   2. Do the same except use symbols.

2. Different chart formats can often be used to portray the same information.

Facts: Three equal size crews are involved doing identical work.   The error quantities for the week are as follows:

Crew A: 20
Crew B: 50
Crew C: 30

Assignment: Depict this information using a:

1.   Pie chart

2.   Bar graph

NOTES

QUIZ

1. In large companies, the data you need is probably in computer storage.

   True_____   False_____

2. Name three general kinds of formats used in the collection of data.

   1._____
   2._____
   3._____

3. Drawings showing the location of defects would be less applicable in a company manufacturing carpeting than one manufacturing hardware.

   True_____   False_____

4. Which technique can precede using a Check List?

   a.   Cause-&-Effect Problem Analysis
   b.   Brainstorming
   c.   Either of the above

5. A job questionnaire generally qualifies as a check sheet.

   True_____   False_____

6. Which technique is most likely to immediately follow the use of a check sheet?

   a.   Cause-&-Effect Problem Analysis
   b.   Pareto chart
   c.   Brainstorming

7. A check sheet helps to assure:

   a. Time will be saved in collecting data
   b. Material collected will be uniformly arranged
   c. Analysis time will be minimized
   d. All of the above

8. The "5 W's and an H" is an example of a memory hook.

   True_____   False_____

9. The facilitator has the responsibility to collect the data needed by the group.

   True_____   False_____

10. It is preferrable to collect slightly more data than you first estimate you will need.

    True_____   False_____

11. Why did you answer question #10 in the way you did?

    _____
    _____
    _____
    _____

12. Occasionally information is collected by posting data onto the check sheet as it occurs.

    True_____   False_____

QUIZ ANSWERS

1. *False, but inquire before collecting it the hard way.*

2. 1. *Check sheets*
    2. *Check lists*
    3. *Drawings showing the location of defects*

3. *False*

4. *Either*

5. *True*

6. *Pareto chart*

7. *All of the above*

8. *True*

9. *False*

10. *True*

11. *Original estimates may prove inadequate. By collecting more than you first estimate is necessary, the "excess" data may save you the trouble of repeating the data collection exercise.*

12. *True*

NOTES

FIFTH MEETING

Welcome the members and guests.

Introduce any guests present.

Have the minutes of the last meeting read and approved.

Review and discuss the material on Data Collection Formats Plus Graphs; and re-do the quiz if helpful.

Discuss any completed worksheet exercises.

Introduce Decision Analysis Using Pareto. Decisions must be made often regarding the data the team collects. The Pareto Chart is a systematic way to do this. It helps to separate the important few from the many trivial items under consideration. Best of all, it does it with a kind of visual impact that convincingly communicates the result to others.

Present the A-V module, stopping where suggested in the manual and elsewhere if helpful.

Get maximum involvement in a discussion of the material presented.

Emphasize that the check sheets used in collecting data often become messy, and the data is often laid out in such a way that it is not readily understandable by simply looking at the information contained thereon. Transferring the data to a chart form corrects this condition. The Pareto chart is easily understood and leaves no doubt as to what decisions must be made.

Talk about the role of the cumulative line. Point out that it is sometimes unnecessary. One use is to graphically calculate the percentage that each column represents of the total. The most important reason for the cumulative line is that it is helpful in the before and after comparison as illustrated in the A-V.

Point out that many people draw a comparison between the Pareto principle and what is often referred to as the 80/20 rule. This rule, which is sometimes described as the 90/10 rule, can be described best with an example. For instance, it could mean that 80% of the errors in an organization are being caused by 20% of the people.

Urge the members to complete the worksheet exercise.

If the team has not yet completed the process of deciding what project to work on, try to get it done at this meeting.

Tell the group that they are about to take on a most challenging assignment -- that of preparing a schedule for carrying out the project selected by them. This comment may evoke reasons why it can't be done at this time because there is not yet adequate information to permit doing it right. However, it is essential to keep in mind that all organizations live by schedules - schedules that were often constructed with sketchy and fragmented pieces of information. The point is, do the best with what is available -- but do it!

Conditions are seldom static! Changes do occur! What if the realities of the schedule are altered? No problem! Simply make the appropriate changes; but label the revised schedule with a number and the date of revision.

Three different schedule formats will be described below. Any one of them can be used, depending on its intended application and on the preference of the members. The first illustration is of the milestone schedule, which is a simplified

version of the milestone chart. It can, under
certain circumstances, become considerably more

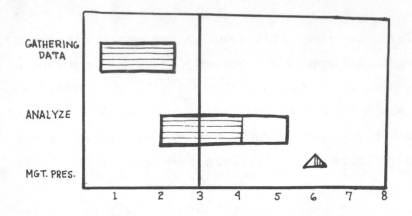

complex as it reflects the totality of the situa-
tion it is portraying.

Next is the line graph schedule, wherein the solid

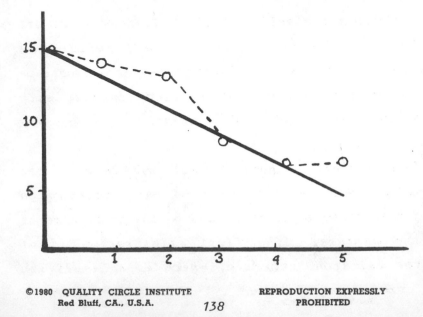

line depicts the plan as perceived when the schedule was conceived, and the dotted line reflects the feedback of results actually being achieved.

The third one is an action plan log, which is basically a schedule. It differs from the two types listed above in that the use of words greatly exceeds the use of graphics. Also, responsibility is more likely to be indicated with this approach.

Each goal (or problem) must be clearly stated. This is very important! Vague statements will hinder progress or make it impossible. An example of an inadequate goal statement might be, "decrease errors." It fails to state specifically what kind of errors and by how much. An improved version is, "decrease typing errors by 20%." Get the members involved in arriving at clear goals statements.

Seldom is a goal attained in a single step. Usually, several Action Steps are required. Involve members in determining what the steps will be. A first step might be, "determine the present error rate." A possible second step could be, "design a check sheet to tally and categorize errors." Subsequent steps might be considered to be solution steps. As with other formats described herein, it is essential to be prepared to revise the action steps as the solution unfolds.

Responsibility must be fixed. Each step in the action plan is assigned to a specific member. If more than one member is needed to be responsible for a particular step, the name of each person must be noted on the log. Occasionally, more than one action step will be assigned to a single member.

If someone outside of the team is identified to help with an action step, the name of the one member who will provide the coordinating link to the assisting non-member must also be listed on the log.

Targeted completion dates are included in the action plan, but they must be agreed to by the persons assigned to carry out the action steps. If you establish the dates, then you own the commitment to meet them rather than the persons assigned to carry out those steps. Target completion dates may change as new facts and circumstances unfold; and the action plan log must be

ACTION ITEMS

| Item | Action | Who | Date | |
			Target	Actual

appropriately up-dated to reflect these changes. The historical value of the log is improved when obsolete dates are lined through rather than erased.

Have the members select the type of schedule they prefer to use and proceed with the scheduling operation.

If sufficient time is available, further the current project.

Suggest that thought be given to the next phase of the current project.

Give the quiz on Decision Analysis Using Pareto.

Suggest that the chapter on Basic Cause & Effect Problem Analysis be read before the next meeting.

Announce the date, place, and time of the next meeting.

Make sure the secretary prepares the minutes.

Confer with your facilitator if required.

CHAPTER SIX

DECISION ANALYSIS USING PARETO

Decisions must be made on a variety of subjects. One decision analysis tool used by teams is the Pareto chart.

☐ Decisions are often difficult to make. The Pareto chart makes the process easier by quantifying the data so that comparisons can be made that are based on facts.

☐ Pareto was a European scholar who lived during the 19th century.

He triggered alarm by graphically depicting the disproportionate distribution of wealth between the various social classes.

☐ Those who talk about the 80-20 rule are referring to the concept of the "major few and the trivial many." For example, 80% of sales may be made by 20% of the salesmen.

Or, 80% of the office errors may be made by 20% of the employees.

☐ 80% of the scrap may be generated by 20% of the work force.

How to
CONSTRUCT

There are several steps in constructing a Pareto chart.

☐ **Step 1.** Determine the time period data is to be collected. Although it may be only a few hours, it may require days or even months.

☐ **Step 2.** Decide what data is to be gathered. Careful consideration at this time will better assure a minimum of trouble later.

Step 3. Design a form that will allow you to collect the data you need. This is your check sheet. Ideally, it should be general enough so that it will allow the information to be arranged in a variety of ways in case the first way fails.

☐ **Step 4.** Record the data on the Check Sheet you have designed.

CHECK SHEET

ERROR	JUNE				TOTAL
	1	2	3	4	
ADDITION	⊞	⊞ ///	⊞ /	⊞ //	27
MULTI-PLICATION	⊞ ⊞ ⊞ ////	⊞ ⊞ ⊞ ///	⊞ ⊞ ///	⊞ ⊞ ⊞	70
OMMISSION	///	⊞ /	//	/	12
ROUTING	//		/	///	6
TYPING	⊞ /	⊞	⊞ /	⊞ //	25
TOTAL	35	42	30	33	140

This is the completed check sheet.

☐ **Step 5.** Refer to the data on the check sheet to construct your Pareto chart.

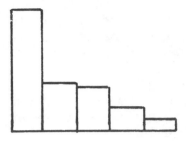

This is the result -- a completed Pareto chart with the columns arranged, as usual, in descending order.

☐   Suppose we were to arrange all the columns in one single tall stack?

It would form a column 140 units high which is also equal to 100%.

☐   Step 6.   This is where we learn how to construct the cumulative or "cum" line.   We know that it reaches a height that is equal to 140 units or 100%.   We will demonstrate how it is constructed.

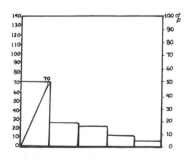

Starting at zero, we extend the cum line to the top right-hand corner of the first column.   It is now at the 70 level.

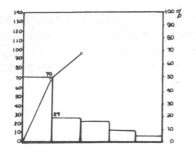

Continue the cum line to a point 27 units higher and directly above the right-hand edge of the second column.

☐ Do the same for the next column of 25 units.

☐ Now you are getting closer as you extend the line for the column of 12 units.

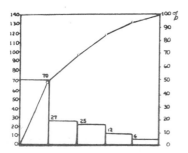

The cum line is complete when it reaches the 100% level per the percentage scale on the right side.

<u>STOP THE A-V</u>

<u>Ask:</u>   *Does each Pareto Chart use a cum line?*

<u>Answer:</u>   *Not every one.*

<u>Comment:</u>   *A prime use is to aid in a before and after comparison. This will be discussed shortly.*

Step 7. Add a legend so that others will not be in the dark when you are not around to answer questions.

☐ There are several points you should remember.

The Pareto chart clearly highlights the number one problem and it does so with visual impact.

☐ The cum line can also be of assistance.

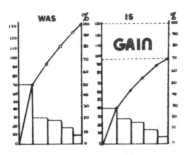

The foremost use of the cum line is to visually compare the before and after situations.

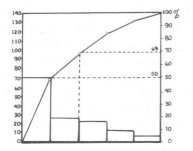

What if you want to determine the percentage of the total that one particular column represents? Draw vertical and horizontal lines as shown by the dotted lines. Easy subtraction provides the answers.

☐ You have just been introduced to the two main reasons why the cumulative line is used by team members.

☐ For many it is just as easy to calculate the percentage using the formula:

$$\frac{\text{Errors in the column: } 27}{\text{Total Errors: } 140} \times 100 = 19+\%$$

☐ What about dollars instead of errors? Thus far, we have discussed Pareto charts that are organized on the basis of errors. At times money is the better choice.

This dramatically illustrates how a minor column might become the major choice when the Pareto chart is arranged by money instead of errors.

CHECK SHEET

ERROR	JUNE 1	2	3	4	TOTAL	WEIGHING FACTOR	WEIGHED TOTAL
ADDITION						27		
MULTIPLICATION						70		
OMMISSION						12		
ROUTING						6		
TYPING						25		
TOTAL	35	42	30	33	140		

Sometimes the analyst must exercise judgment based on his specialized knowledge of the subject. For example, he may look at a check sheet containing defect information and decide to assign priorities to each item. To do this we have added two columns to the right as shown.

CHECK SHEET

ERROR	JUNE 1	2	3	4	TOTAL	WEIGHING FACTOR	WEIGHED TOTAL
ADDITION						27	1	
MULTIPLICATION						70	1	
OMMISSION						12	3	
ROUTING						6	2	
TYPING						25	1	
TOTAL	35	42	30	33	140		

Add the weighting factors. One (1) is the weighting factor for items you do not want to change. The more importance you attach, the greater the weighting factor.

CHECK SHEET

ERROR	JUNE 1	2	3	4	TOTAL	WEIGHING FACTOR	WEIGHED TOTAL
ADDITION						27	1	27
MULTIPLICATION						70	1	70
OMMISSION						12	3	36
ROUTING						6	2	12
TYPING						25	1	25
TOTAL	35	42	30	33	140		170

Multiply each category of error by the weighting factor to get the new weighted total. In this instance the number problem remained the top one. Occasionally, this technique will cause change in the order of priorities.

☐ What are some of the reasons weighting factors are used? No one wants an unhappy customer. Know what your customer places the greatest value on and respond accordingly.

☐ Urgency is another reason you might decide to use weighting factors. Two examples might be legal considerations or governmental pressures.

<u>STOP THE A-V</u>

<u>Comment:</u>   *The use of weighting factors can be helpful in decision analysis. However, keep in mind that judgment is involved and members may be asked to justify their weighting selections.*

<u>Ask:</u>   *What can be done to assure that the weighting selections can be justified?*

<u>Answer:</u> 1.   *Ask for advice from someone who qualifies as an "expert."*
          2.   *Inform the manager of the logic you are using.*
          3.   *If available, use historical precedents.*

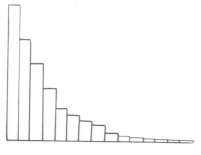

Occasionally a Pareto chart may contain a large number of columns.

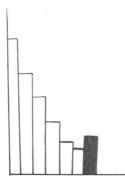

Often, the trivial columns are lumped together under one column titled, "other." Watch out! Do not "bury" and forget a small but extremely important column this way.

☐   Stratification generally means to separate out or rearrange data to find more meaningful ways to present it.

☐   How do we arrange the data in the most mean-ingful way possible? Careful thought must be given to this important process. In Step 2 we selected the category we wished to use to arrange our data. In it we used "errors" and it was quite satisfactory.

Arranging it by "errors" could have taken on this appearance. No category stands out. Perhaps it should be arranged by the originating work unit.

Grouped by "originating work unit" is no improvement. Still no column stands out. Let's try arranging by the shift it was done on.

Organizing it by shift proves successful! One column boldly stands out to indicate that the 3rd shift is the source of our problem. At this point you might immediately do a second Pareto Chart dealing with errors on the third shift only.

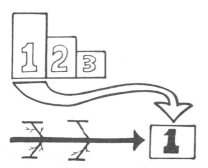

Here is a question. After the Pareto chart has identified the major problem, then what? That number 1 problem is then subjected to Cause-&-Effect Analysis to find the true cause.

☐ We are now set to look at practical applications of this decision analysis technique.

☐ For example, electro-mechanical subassemblies are being rejected for a variety of reasons. The investigation led to the creation of two successive and related Pareto charts.

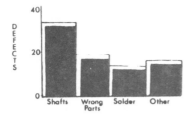

This first Pareto chart was constructed and conclusively demonstrated that the shafts were the biggest reasons for the units being rejected.

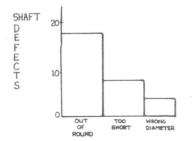

The second Pareto chart was used to focus in on shaft defects only. It resulted in the finding that most shafts were out-of-round.

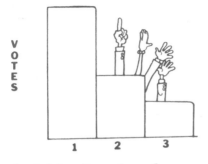

Peridically, brainstorming is employed to identify a list of possible themes. The team must then prioritize its top selections. This is most usually done by a voting process. The size of the vote controls the height of each column.

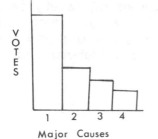

Occasionally, members do the same thing to the major causes identified by Cause-&-Effect Problem Analysis.

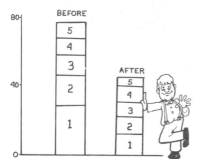

This is another variation on how to present a before and after comparison. Simply stack the columns of the two Pareto charts.

☐ Pareto charts can be posted in the work area to keep employees informed.

☐ Management presentations are more effective when visual aids, such as Pareto charts, are displayed.

☐ There are endless applications for this versatile tool.

The number of safety days without an accident for each work group can be shown on a Pareto chart.

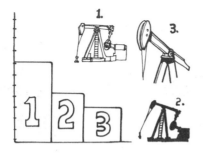

Oil well production can be illustrated on a Pareto chart.

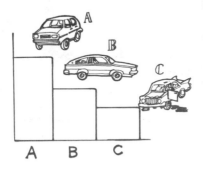

Some automobiles hold their value better than others as this chart suggests. Pareto charts can be a most effective way to make decisions on a variety of topics. It's a good idea to use this valuable time-proven technique.

WORK SHEET

1. Pareto charts help us to visualize alternatives. They are constructed using information gathered on a check sheet.

   Assignment: (1) Refer back to the check sheet you created in question #1 of Work Sheet Exercise-Data Collection Forms, & Graphs. Using this check sheet, construct a Pareto chart. (2) Add in the cumulative line.

2. Sometimes in doing decision analysis we wish to add weighting factors to keep things in relative perspective.

Facts: Two types of errors are considered more significant than others. Therefore, they are weighted as follows:

Error	Weight
* Incomplete address	2
* Delivered to wrong party	3

Assignment: (1) Add a weighting column to the check sheet used in question #1. Add another column to the right of it titled, "Weighted Total."

(2) Construct another Pareto chart on the basis of this new information.

(3) Draw in the cumulative line.

QUIZ

1. Each Pareto chart must use the "other" column to reduce the number of minor columns.

2. Theoretically, the maximum number of columns a Pareto chart can have is,

   a. Six
   b. Ten
   c. No limit

3. Theoretically, the minimum number of columns a Pareto chart can have is,

   a. Two
   b. Three
   c. Four

4. The cumulative line can be used to graphically calculate the percentage each column represents of the total.

   True_____   False_____

5. The cumulative line makes before and after comparisons easier to visualize.

   True_____   False_____

6. Normally, what precedes constructing a Pareto chart?

   a. Cause-&-Effect Problem Analysis
   b. Check sheet
   c. Brainstorming

7. Normally, what technique follows the Pareto chart?

    a. Cause-&-Effect Problem Analysis
    b. Brainstorming
    c. Check sheet

8. The use of the cumulative line is:

    a. Mandatory
    b. Recommended for some appllications
    c. Rarely used

9. The columns can be arranged in descending order from left to right or vice versa.

    True_____   False_____

10. It may be advantageous to arrange the columns of a Pareto chart by dollar amounts instead of by quantity of defects.

    True_____   False_____

11. Are the columns of a Pareto chart ever arranged by "urgency?"

    True_____   False_____

12. There are instances where the results of one Pareto chart can immediately trigger a second Pareto chart.

    True_____   False_____

QUIZ ANSWERS

1.   False

2.   No limit

3.   Two

4.   True

5.   True

6.   Check sheet

7.   Cause-&-Effect Problem Analysis

8.   Recommended for some applications

9.   False.   This applies particularly when the cumulative line is used.

10. True

11. Yes

12. True

NOTES

SIXTH MEETING

Welcome the members and guests.

Introduce any guests present.

Have the minutes of the last meeting read and approved.

Review and discuss the material on Decision Analysis Using Pareto; and re-do the quiz if helpful.

Discuss any completed worksheet exercises.

Introduce Basic Cause & Effect Problem Analysis. Explain that after the Pareto Analysis has identified the number one problem, it must be subjected to a special type of further analysis which will help to determine the true cause of that problem.

Ask the members to notice how a technique which was previously learned, Brainstorming, plays an important part in Basic Cause & Effect Analysis. In effect, they will see how this system transforms the Brainstorming into a special type of picture, sometimes called a fishbone diagram, where similar ideas are grouped together. This speeds the completion of the subsequent steps where the analytical techniques are applied to arrive at the true cause.

Present the A-V module, stopping where suggested in the manual and elsewhere if helpful.

Get maximum involvement in a discussion of the material presented. Remind the members that problems are to be stated as precisely as possible if they are to save time and to maximize the likelihood of success. Selection of the major groupings should not be limited to the 4Ms. If other groupings are appropriate, use them. You may want to ask members if they have examples of other groupings that could be used.

During the brainstorming step, use abbreviations of words and sentences whenever possible; but it is essential that the person originating the idea agrees with the abbreviation used.

Apply Roberts or other Rules of Order whenever someone wants to advance an argument for or against the cause to be voted on. When all discussion has ended, the vote can then be taken on that particular cause.

Remind members that the Cause & Effect diagram can also be used as a teaching device. The effect might be stated as a properly built unit or, if in an office, a properly processed piece of paper-work. The causes, or items contributing to the desired end would be listed during the brain-storming session. This exercise alerts employees, new or experienced, on the many factors that must be considered to produce error free output.

Here is an exercise that the group will enjoy. Ask each member to take off his or her wristwatch without looking at it and put it out of sight. Then remind them of the importance of change in helping to zero in on the true cause. Talk about how our minds can help us in this regard! Our brains tend to filter out everything that is commmonplace; but they help us by remembering that which has changed.

To illustrate how this works, remind the members that the watches they have just put aside have got to be one of the most familiar objects they own; because they must surely look at them a great number of times each day. Therefore, they should be able to describe them in great detail.

Then, get each in turn to fully describe his or

her wristwatch. The results are good for a lot of laughs; because few people will be able to even come close. Some will put numbers where none exist. Some will not be able to remember the brand names. Remind them that the only thing they see is what has changed, which is the time. The mind has filtered out everything that remains unchanged.

Urge the members to complete the worksheet exercise.

Now go to work on the current project. Ideally, you would apply Basic Cause & Effect Problem Analysis to it at this time; but it may not be at the appropriate stage for this. If this is the case, you might try a sample Cause & Effect project that can involve all of the members. If the alloted time is short, you might shorten the various steps involved. For example, during the brainstorming step, yu could limit it to only two rounds of ideas.

Be sure to post your project schedule and make any required adjustments.

Suggest that the members be thinking about the current team project.

Give the quiz on Basic Cause & Effect Problem Analysis.

Suggest that the chapter on Process Cause & Effect Problem Analysis be read before the next meeting.

Announce the date, time, and place of the next meeting.

Thank attendees for their attention and cooperation.

Make sure the secretary prepares the minutes.

Confer with your facilitator, if required.

NOTES

CHAPTER SEVEN

BASIC CAUSE & EFFECT PROBLEM ANALYSIS

The primary purpose of this technique is to help you solve problems.

☐ The problem is the effect and is written in the box to the right. The possible causes for the problem are written in the area to the left.

You may have wondered why some call it a "fish bone diagram." One look at your first completed Cause-&-Effect Problem Analysis will show you why.

☐ Too often it is the boss who personally attempts to solve all the problems in his area.

☐ Sometimes the staff people are asked to do it.

☐ What about getting the people who are doing the hands-on work to get involved?

You would not go to a barber if you had a toothache. It makes common sense to take problems to the experts. In your organization, no one is more expert about the job than the person actually doing it.

☐ Members select a problem to analyze from within their areas of work responsibility. Several steps are involved.

1.

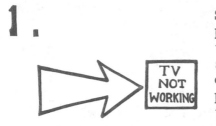

Step 1 is to state the problem. In this case the problem is a television set that doesn't operate properly. When possible, try to define the problem as precisely as possible.

☐ If, for instance, you know that the sound is absent, so state it in your definition of the problem. This knowledge will assure more accurate pinpointing of possible causes. The net effect should be a savings in time to solve the problem.

☐ Whenever you work, always refrain from trying to solve the "other" person's problems. Remember, you are not the expert once you leave your area of specialty.

STOP THE A-V

Ask: *There seems to be wisdom in having an expert analyze the problem. How does that principle apply here?*

Answer: 1. *The employees doing the work know more about it than anyone else.*

2. *Problems should be selected in ones own area of expertise.*

Comment: *That does not mean that one never looks outside of his or her own area. After experience has been gained, it is possible that two groups will work together on a joint problem.*

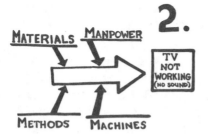

2. In Step 2 is where you determine the major groupings for the possible causes that will be identified. Any number of such groupings is permissable, although three or four are quite common. The 4 M's: materials, manpower, methods, and machines, are favorites.

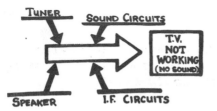

More experienced groups are likely to consider incorporating major groupings more specifically taylored to fit the problem.

3.

In Step 3 all members get involved by participating in a brainstorming session.

☐ Brainstorming works best when certain rules are followed. The leader reviews these prior to each session.

☐ Each member, in rotation, is asked for ideas. This continues until all ideas are brought out.

☐ A member may have several ideas but can offer only one per turn.

☐ When no idea occurs, simply say, "Pass."

☐ No idea should be treated as stupid. Ideas are not to be evaluated during the brainstorming session.

☐ An explosion of ideas is better assured when you approach your task by thinking in terms of the 5 W's and 1 H.

Exaggeration often adds a creative stimulus to brainstorming.

☐ When the rules have been explained, the team can commence the brainstorming process.

☐ The process is speeded substantially by the leader asking a member to write the ideas as they are given.

☐ A member should indicate the major grouping he wishes his idea included under. For example, he should say, "Under Manpower, 'Attitudes'."

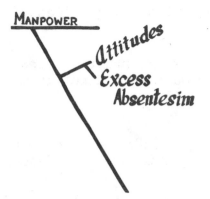

Occasionally a cause can be added as a branch off a cause already on the chart. It should be stated as, "Under Manpower, as a branch off of 'Attitudes' put 'excess absenteeism'."

☐ The picture of the completed brainstorming session should show similar ideas grouped together in clumps. Thus, it will be simpler to analyze.

☐ The brainstorming is over when everyone says, "Pass."

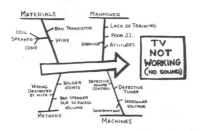

The Cause and Effect diagram may look like this at that time.

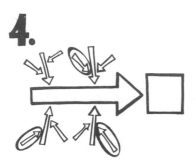

In Step 4, the ideas collected during brainstorming are critically examined to identify those that are best.

☐ Identifying the best causes can be a time consuming process involving a criticl analysis of the pros and cons of each.

☐ Or, you can speed the process immeasureably by giving members the opportunity to vote for each cause they believe to be important. It may not seem scientific but experience has demonstrated that it works quite well.

LACK OF TRAINING 4

POOR J.I. 8

SABATOGE 2

ATTITUDES

The leader informs members they can vote for as many of the ideas as they wish. The leader begins by pointing to one of the causes and asking, for example, "How many wish to vote for 'Lack of Training'?" The vote, in this case, 4 is recorded on the diagram. This procedure is followed until all causes have been voted on. When no votes are received, simply draw a line through that cause.

☐ Next, those with the highest number of votes are circled. Usually this means at least two and up to five or six but there is no set number.

In this instance the three causes receiving the maximum number of votes were circled.

When examining each cause, look for something that has changed. Few things serve as better clues.

☐ <u>Look for deviations from the norm.</u> If one's weight shoots up unexpectedly, it might tie into an accompanyng variation in diet or exercise patterns.

☐ Police look for clues of recurring "patterns" that will help them in identifying criminals. "Patterns" are useful tools in any field of problem analysis.

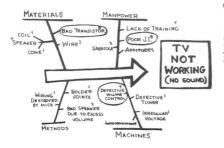

This is the Cause-&-Effect diagram with the major causes circled. Now you can focus in on just a few causes — much less confusing!

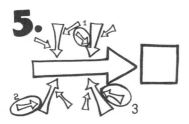

In Step 5, the most probable causes will be ranked in order of importance.

☐ To do this, look only at those causes that have been circled.

☐ Ask members to vote only on these major causes.

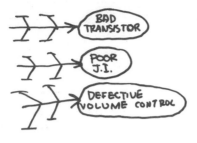

Will the choice be difficult? Need more insight into one or more of the circled causes? If so, a special analysis can be done with the circled cause as the effect. Everything else is identical. Normally, this special step is not taken but circumstances may warrant it.

☐ Regardless of whether it is used or not, finally the voting begins. Write the number of votes beside each major cause.

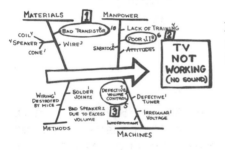

Finally, add the priority ranking beside each of the major causes.

☐ In Steps 5 and 6, do we simply vote or can we first argue for or against any of the causes? A member can halt the voting on any issue to speak out. Others may support or oppose him. Only then will the voting take place. This can occur in either Step 4 or Step 5.

☐ Sometimes the results of this phase of the voting are arranged into a Pareto chart. The height of each column reflects the way the voting went. Usually this is done with the intent to use it in their management presentation.

STOP THE A-V

> Ask: In what way does the voting assist in analyzing a problem?
>
> Answers: 1. It speeds the process.
> 2. Everyone is involved.
>
> Comment: Discussion to evaluate the pros and cons is encouraged at any time during voting.

6. In Step 6, the one most likely cause is tested in an attempt to verify it. This step may be easy in the case of most TV repairs, or, occasionally difficult and time consuming. But, it must always be done.

☐ The top cause is labeled #1. That is the one we want to attempt to verify.

☐ A good way to do this is a brainstorming session. Members are asked for their suggestions.

☐ Airplane manufacturers minimize the cost of verification by using models. Whatever your team selects as a verification test, try it to see if it supports your conclusions.

RECOMMENDED SOLUTIONS

There is an important follow-up to the Cause-&-Effect Problem Analysis: The Recommended Solution.

- ☐ Cause-&-Effect Problem Analysis aids in discovering and verifying the true cause of the problem Then, you can prepare a Recommended Solution.

- ☐ Member involvement is encouraged in identifying various ways to correct the problem -- an excellent opportunity to utilize the brainstorming technique.

- ☐ The pros and cons of the top alternatives are debated by the members to achieve a concensus. Maybe it's a choice between "Replace" and "Repair."

- ☐ The recommended solution becomes part of the presentation to management.

Cause-&-Effect Problem Analysis is usually employed to solve problems. However, a couple of other applications should be considered.

Occasionally we are pleasantly surprised when something unexpectedly takes a turn for the better. Unless we find out why this occurred, it may resume its former characteristics just as suddenly. Use Cause-&-Effect Analysis to find the cause of this "good" problem.

Some leaders have found Cause-&-Effect diagrams to be an excellent teaching device. The effect might be, for example, "The Job Description." The brainstorming session would be where members suggest all those things that cause it to be right.

ACTION ITEMS

Item	Action	Who	Date	
			Target	Actual

Want results? Identify problems or objectives and specify the action needed. State who will follow through and set a target date for completion.

There are some items to remember when using this versatile tool.

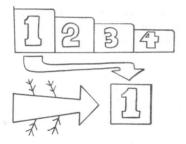

The problem you have selected often comes as a result of Pareto Analysis.

☐ "Leader directed" Cause-&-Effect Problem Analysis is sometimes used to help prioritize the most likely circled causes during Step 5. This technique will be explained in detail during your study cf Process Cause-&-Effect Problem Analysis; but it is just as applicable here.

Earlier we pointed to the value of watching for changes or deviations as important clues. Members are encouraged to call out such additional information as dates, sizes, and extent. Post it to your diagram.

☐ The leader writes the ideas so that everyone can see them and where there can be a permanent record. This is possible with either a large sheet of paper or a vu-graph projector. Avoid note pads or a blackboard.

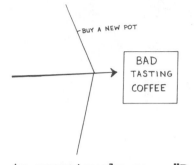

During the brainstorming step, some members tend to jump ahead and state "solutions" rather than possible causes. It is too early to assume that the true cause has been identified. In the problem of bad tasting coffee it would be wrong to prematurely say, "Buy a new pot."

☐ Simply state it as a possible cause, such as, "Defective coffee pot."

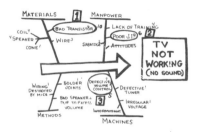

Use the original Cause-&-Effect chart when doing the management presentation. Its realism carries more impact than one that has been neatly re-done.

☐ You are not finished until you record on the diagram a legend that gives information such as a date, the group that did it, and the name of the leader.

NOTES

WORK SHEET

1. Cause-&-Effect Problem Analysis aids us in identifying the true cause of a problem (or effect). The problem you wish to analyze is "Heat Cost." You have gathered your family together to do a Cause-&-Effect Analysis.

   <u>Assignment:</u> Go through all the steps as follows:

   1. State the problem as precisely as possible. The words "Heat Cost" could mean several things, for example; in the fireplace, the kitchen range, the basement, the attic, or the house in total. The time of year could also be a significant factor. Use your imagination and be precise.

   2. Identify the major cause groupings. Use the 4 M's if you wish, or some other variation.

   3. Brainstorm to identify possible causes. Use your imagination.

   4. Use a voting procedure and discussion to identify the most likely causes. Circle the ones getting the highest number of votes.

   5. Prioritize the causes just circled by using a voting and discussion procedure.

   6. Verification. Get everyones involvement to find an appropriate test to see if it can be verified that the number one cause is truly responsible.

   7. Solution. Briefly describe the action you would initiate to correct the problem.

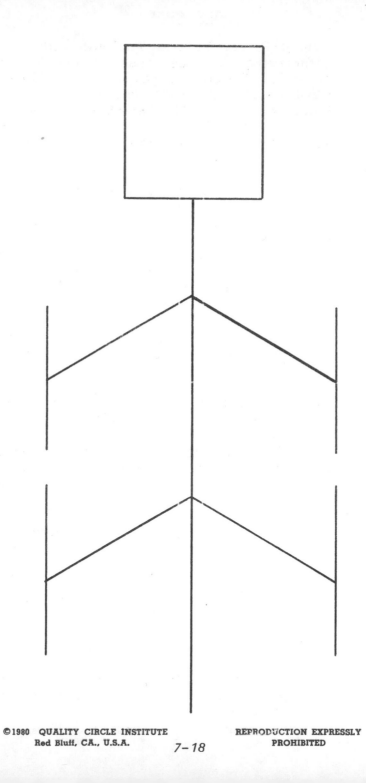

7-18

QUIZ

1. The problem to be analyzed should be kept somewhat general in scope as to encourage a broad range of possible causes to be suggested.

    True_____   False_____

2. Preceeding the brainstorming step of Cause-&-Effect Problem Analysis, the rules of brainstorming should be reviewed only when new members or visitors are present.

    True_____   False_____

3. Can you name the 4 M's?

4. Suggested causes must have relevance to the problem. Otherwise, it is preferrable not to list them.

    True_____   False_____

5. Cause-&-Effect Problem Analysis must always be led by the leader.

    True_____   False_____

6. During the Step where causes are evaluated, how many should be circled?

    a.   One
    b.   Three
    c.   No theoretical limit

7. When seeking the most likely causes certain types of clues will be especially helpful. Several answers apply.

    a.   Changes
    b.   Similarities

c. Recurring pattern
d. Causes suggested by visiting staff personnel
e. Causes that generate the most discussion
f. Notable distinctions

8. Discussion of the suggested causes can take place:

   a. During brainstorming
   b. During voting to determine the most likely possible causes
   c. During the verification step

9. The verification step in Cause-&-Effect Problem Analysis is:

   a. Mandatory
   b. Recommended
   c. Seldom used

10. Normally, the technique that immediately proceeds Cause-&-Effect Problem Analysis is:

    a. Brainstorming
    b. Check sheet
    c. Pareto chart

11. In order of preference, the Cause-&-Effect Problem Analysis should be done on a:

    a.____Blackboard
    b.____Note pad
    c.____Large sheet of paper
    d.____Overhead projector

QUIZ ANSWERS

1. False. The more specifically the problem is stated, the greater the potential for a rapid and successful analysis.

2. False

3. Manpower, methods, materials, and machinery

4. False. Relevance is not discussed during the brainstorming step.

5. False

6. No theoretical limit.

7. Changes,
   similarities,
   recurring patterns,
   notable distinctions

8. During voting to determine the most likely possible causes.

9. Mandatory

10. Pareto chart

11. <u>1</u> Large sheet of paper. It can be seen by all and it provides a permanent record.

   <u>2</u> Overhead projector. Same.

   <u>3</u> Black board. It can be seen but must be copied to have a record.

   <u>4</u> Note pad. It provides a record, but because it cannot be seen, ideas tend to be repeated. Also, new ideas tend to be reduced.

NOTES

SEVENTH MEETING

Welcome members and guests.

Introduce any guests present.

Have the minutes of the last meeting read and approved.

Review and discuss the material on Basic Cause & Effect Problem Analysis; and re-do the quiz if helpful.

Discuss any completed worksheet exercises.

Introduce Process C & E Problem Analysis. Tell the members that this is an interesting variation of Basic Cause & Effect Problem Analysis that can often lead to the more rapid solution of problems. Its key feature is that each step in the process is identified and is analyzed separately. It is essential to carefully review what was learned in Basic Cause & Effect Problem Analysis before proceeding to this new approach.

Present the A-V module, stopping where suggested in the manual and elsewhere if helpful.

Get maximum involvement in a discussion of the material presented. In Process C & E Problem Analysis, it is not necessary to analyze the blocks in sequence. By the time the blocks have been defined, understanding of the problem may be so clear that it is unnecessary to start with the first block and proceed through each of the others. That is, the members may feel confident that they have isolated the problem in one particular block. After identifying the most likely cause, attempt to verify it. If successful, it may not be necessary to do the other blocks.

Point out that in Process C & E Problem Analysis, you can brainstorm between blocks, if necessary, to deal adequately with something that was left out earlier. An example might be a block called "transportation." If it had been recognized in the beginning, it would have been assigned its own block. It is just as important to define the problem as specifically as possible in Step One of Process C & E Problem Analysis as it is in Step One of Basic.

Urge members to complete the worksheet exercise.

Go to work on the current project. If possible, apply Process C & E Problem Analysis. If this is impractical, apply it to a fictitious problem so that the members can have a chance to use this new technique. If time is limited, limit the time spent on the brainstorming phase.

Post the project schedule and revise it, if necessary.

Suggest that members be thinking about the next phase of the current project.

Give the quiz on Process C & E Problem Analysis.

Suggest that the chapter on The Management Presentation be read before the next meeting.

Announce the date, time, and place of the next meeting.

Thank the attendees for their attention and cooperation.

Make sure the secretary prepares the minutes.

Confer with your facilitator if required.

NOTES

CHAPTER EIGHT

PROCESS CAUSE & EFFECT PROBLEM ANALYSIS

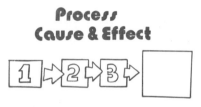

Process
Cause & Effect

Problem Analysis

Process Cause-&-Effect Problem Analysis provides a way to use this valuable technique in a most effective manner.

☐ Before explaining this variation, let us quickly review the Basic Cause-&-Effect technique.

☐ Step 1. Write the problem as precisely as possible in the block to the right and draw an arrow pointing to it.

□ In Step 2 you lay the groundwork for organizing the upcoming brainstorming step. Determine the major cause groupings. The 4 M's are
often suited for this purpose.

□ Step 3 is the brainstorming session in which
all members participate by suggesting possible
causes of the problem.

□ In Step 4 the most significant causes are
identified. They are then highlighted by
circling them.

□ In Step 5 the most likely causes are prioritized in order of importance.

□ Step 6 is the process by which the number one
choice is tested in some way to verify or
disprove it.

Here is what the com-
pleted diagram looks
like.

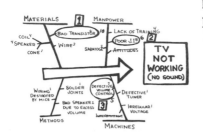

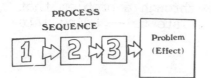

Process Cause-&-Effect Problem Analysis is similar in some respects to Basic Cause-&-Effect Problem Analysis. There are, however, some important differences.

☐ The process involves several steps.

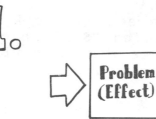

In Step 1 the problem is identified as precisely as possible. (No difference here from Basic Cause-&-Effect Problem Analysis.)

In Step 2 the process sequence is determined.

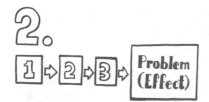

☐ Usually, the process sequence begins with the first step and those that follow are taken one-at-a-time.

☐ But, sometimes it is easier to work backwards.

☐   For example let's work through a problem that just might be easy to relate to -- being late for work!

The first block in the sequence is easy. We label it "Get Ready" and it includes what we do from the time we wake up until we are dressed.

The second block is labeled "EAT" and it covers what takes place at breakfast.

The final block in the sequence is labeled "DRIVE", to describe the task of driving to work.

☐   An example in an office might be the excessive delays in the flow of certain paperwork. The sequence or flow of work can be identified easily. First, a draft is prepared. Next, it is typed. Finally, it is mailed.

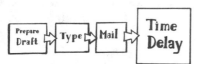

The sequence is depicted graphically in this Process Cause-&-Effect illustration.

☐ This process is just as applicable in a factory. For example, let's assume that the metal is not adhering properly in a plating department. The sequence might be: First, dip the parts in the plating tank; second, dip them in a rinsing tank, and, finally air dry them.

This process is depicted by this Process Cause-&-Effect Problem Analysis.

STOP THE A-V

Ask: Are the blocks in the process arranged in any special sequence?

Answer: Yes, in the sequence they happen.

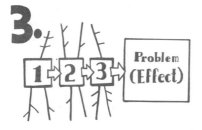

Step 3 is the brainstorming session where all members of the team get involved in suggesting possible causes.

☐ Brainstorming is most productive when certain rules are followed. These are explained in detail in the section entitled, "Brainstorming." In general, they include "go in rotation," "only one idea per person," and, "no criticism during this phase."

☐ After the rules have been explained, the members can commence the brainstorming process.

☐ The process moves at a much faster pace when the leader is assisted by a member who writes down the ideas as they are called out.

☐ Back to the first example. Concentrate only on the block titled, "Get Up." Use brainstorming to identify possible causes for being late to work.

☐ When you complete the first block in the sequence, move to "EAT" and do the same.

Then move to the final block in the sequence. The brainstorming is completed when each person says, "Pass."

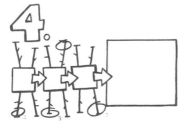

Step 4 is where the ideas collected during brainstorming are critically examined to select those that are best.

☐ Each cause must be evaluated to determine its degree of merit. This may involve considerable time and detailed analysis.

☐ However, time is a luxury usually in short supply. Voting is comparatively rapid and the results are usually impressive.

The leader instructs members that they may vote for as many ideas as they wish. The leader begins by pointing to one of the causes and asking, for example, "How many wish to vote for 'Lack of training'?" The vote, in this example, is 4, and is recorded on the diagram. Continue until all causes have been voted on. When no votes are received, simply draw a line through that cause.

☐ Next, those with the highest number of votes are circled. Usually this means at least two or three, but could include more.

In this example, three causes receiving the most votes are circled.

☐ Anything that has changed serves as an excellent clue to discovering the true cause.

☐ Likewise, deviations from the norm also function as clues.

☐ Police realize that "recurring patterns" are excellent clues.

This is the diagram showing the major causes circled.

5.

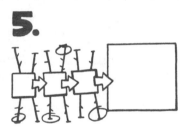

In Step 5 the causes highlighted in Step 4 are ranked in order of importance. To accomplish this, examine only those causes that have been circled.

☐ Each cause that is circled will be voted on.

☐ Ask members to vote <u>only</u> on these major causes.

☐ Jot down the number of votes next to each circled cause.

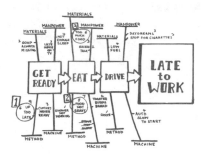

Then rank each in accordance with the number of votes received.

☐ A member may halt the voting at any time to argue for or against any cause. This can occur in either Step 4 or Step 5.

☐ Sometimes the results are arranged in Pareto chart fashion to spotlight the results. This may be done so as to use this chart in the management presentation.

In Step 6, the number one most likely cause is testd in an attempt to verify it. Perhaps the alarm must be set to go off earlier!

☐ The number one cause is the one we want to verify.

A good way to do this is a brainstorming session to get the ideas of all members.

☐ Airplane manufacturers minimize the cost of verification by using models.

☐ There is an important follow-up to the verification process: The Recommended Solution.

☐ Use brainstorming to get member involvement in identifying various solution alternatives.

☐ The pros and cons of the top alternatives are debated by the members to achieve a consensus.

☐ The selected solution becomes part of the management presentation.

There are several things to remember.

THINGS TO REMEMBER

8-10

☐ During the brainstorming phase, concentrate on one block at a time rather than scattering the groups thoughts by jumping back-and-forth.

☐ Let us review how you might save time and effort during brainstorming. It may be quite obvious that one block is the source of the true cause.

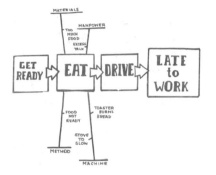

We will assume that you want to focus in on the block titled, "EAT." Therefore, center your brainstorming in this area only.

☐ Proceed to Step 4 and Step 5 while continuing to focus in on the same block.

STOP THE A-V

Ask: Why would you concentrate on one block only?

Answers: 1. Because the probability is very high that it contains the true cause.
2. It will save time.

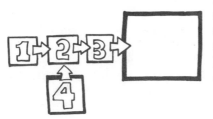

The blocks are usually in sequence but occasionally one of the blocks is offset if that reflects how the process actually occurs.

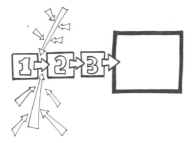

It is possible that the members will decide to brainstorm what may have occurred during transportation between blocks. Do it in the manner indicated. If this step had been anticipated earlier, it could have been added as a separate

block!

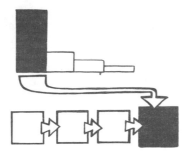

And, of course, although it may be very basic, the problem you have selected for analysis often came about after using Pareto analysis to select it.

☐ "Leader directed" Cause-&-Effect Problem Analysis is sometimes a very valuable variation that can be applied to <u>either</u> type of Cause-&-Effect analysis.

☐   As you will recall, in Step 5, voting is used to prioritize the major causes that have been circled. But, prior to the vote, the members may want a clearer understanding of one or more of the choices. So, the leader assumes control by asking a series of "Why, When, Where, Who, What, and How" questions that anyone may answer.

To illustrate, let us look at a major cause entitled, "No Training."

The leader asks, "Why is no training provided?" A member responds, "We don't ever have a classroom."

The leader questions, "Why is there no classroom?" A different member answers, "It has never been budgeted."

CLASSROOM NOT AVAILABLE
NO BUDGET
MGR. OPPOSED
NO TRAINING

The leader asks, "Why?" The answer comes back, "The boss opposes it." This line of questioning can be continued for some time. It is an excellent way to expose the smallest details. Thus, the group can be much more informed and confident as it proceeds with the vote on whether "no training" is the true cause.

☐ Finally, in the event your work is referred to at some future date, include a legend. It makes a document even more valuable.

WORK SHEET

1. Process Cause-&-Effect can be used to advantage where several sequencial steps occur. Such is the case in the problem of "Poor Tasting Meal."

   <u>Assignment:</u> Using the problem "Poor Tasting Meal", identify the blocks that are involved in the entire sequence. If you wish, to get started, use for your first block "Purchase Meal Ingredients."

   → POOR TASTING MEAL

2. The process of identifying each block in the sequence often lends enough insight that one specific block is chosen to initiate the brainstorming.

   <u>Assignment:</u> In your case, what block would you brainstorm first? Why?

3. Leader-directed Cause-&-Effect often proves effective in expanding our insight into one of the major causes that has been circled. Let us say such a major cause is "Lack of Training."

   <u>Assignment:</u> Assume you are the leader. Ask a series of at least three questions to open up (expand) "Lack of Training." Also, use your imagination to supply possible answers you might receive.

   <u>Question</u>   <u>Response</u>

   1.

   2.

   3.

QUIZ

1. Name the two major types of Cause-&-Effect Problem Analysis.

   1._____
   2._____

2. Cause-&-Effect Problem Analysis is just as effective for office and technical operations as it is for manufacturing areas.

   True_____   False_____

3. Leader directed Cause-&-Effect is as applicable for Basic Cause-&-Effect as it is for Process Cause-&-Effect.

   True_____   False_____

4. When voting on the most likely causes, to avoid dissention, it is preferrable not to allow discussion.

   True_____   False_____

5. A precise statement of the problem to be analyzed is the task of the leader. Member involvement occurs only after brainstorming starts.

   True_____   False_____

6. In Process Cause-&-Effect, the identification and sequence of the blocks precedes the statement of the problem.

   True_____   False_____

7. In Process Cause-&-Effect, it is not mandatory to brainstorm each block in the same sequence the work is done.

   True_____   False_____

8. Discussion of all the ideas suggested during brainstorming should take place prior to voting, not during the actual process.

   True_____   False_____

9. Leader-directed Cause-&-Effect can be used during the brainstorming step to get things moving. Once things get rolling the leader should return to the normal type of brainstorming.

   True_____   False_____

10. Leader-directed Cause-&-Effect is usually most effective when "expanding" some or all of the circled causes to gain in-depth insight into each cause prior to voting.

   True_____   False_____

11. In Process Cause-&-Effect, during the brainstorming step, ideas may be directed at any block in the process. In other words, it is not necessary to brainstorm one block at a time.

   True_____   False_____

12. In Process Cause-&-Effect, it is mandatory to brainstorm all remaining blocks even though the group is certain it has discovered the true cause.

   True_____   False_____

QUIZ ANSWERS

1. 1) Basic
    2) Process

2. True

3. True

4. False. Discussion should be encouraged.

5. False. Get member involvement in precisely stating the problem.

6. False. The problem is stated first.

7. True

8. False. It will save an enormous amount of time to discuss only ideas the members want to explore or offer opinions on before voting. After the top vote getters are circled, then discuss all of them, pro and con, prior to your final vote.

9. True

10. True

11. False. It is preferrable to concentrate everyone's energy on one block at a time.

12. False. It may prove helpful but time constraints may not allow this to easily occur.

NOTES

EIGHTH MEETING

Welcome members and guests.

Introduce any guests present.

Have the minutes of the last meeting read and approved.

Review and discuss Process C & E Problem Analysis; and re-do the quiz if helpful.

Discuss any completed worksheet exercises.

Introduce The Management Presentation. Point out the importance of being able to communicate with all levels and functions of an organization. Management looks for proof of the need to implement a recommendation. An effective, proven way to convince them is to use charts, pictures, and actual examples. The members must learn to speak management's language in order to better assure the approval of their recommendations.

Present the A-V module, stopping when suggested in the manual and elsewhere if helpful.

Get maximum involvement in a discussion of the

material presented. Point out that questions and answers are encouraged both during and after a management presentation.

Call attention to the KISS principle (keep it sweet and simple) as a basic way to assure clear communication. Stress the importance of enhancing the communication process with lettering on the various charts that can be easily read.

The group should be made to understand that each one of them will have the opportunity to take part in the presentation when it is made. Each will have two to three minutes in which to speak.

Advise the members that you will let them know weeks in advance of an actual presentation, so that they can have plenty of time to prepare for it. You will also try to have a photographer take pictures for possible use in your organization's own publication.

Urge members to complete the worksheet exercise.

Turn attention now to furthering the team's current project.

Post the project schedule and alter it if necessary.

Suggest that the members be thinking about the next phase of the current project.

Give the quiz on The Management Presentation.

Announce the date, time, and place of the next meeting.

Thank the attendees for their attention and cooperation.

Make sure the secretary prepares the minutes.

Confer with your facilitator, if required.

NOTES

CHAPTER NINE

THE MANAGEMENT PRESENTATION

The management presentation is an important and rewarding feature of your activities. This section is designed to prepare you to carry off this technique in the most effective way possible.

☐ It may be the first time you have had the opportunity to present your ideas to management.

☐ The presentation is a team effort. Everyone has participated in the analysis and evryone is encouraged to take part in the presentation.

Communication is a prime reason for the management presentation.

☐ Why not simply submit a written recommendation? Prime reasons include: it may be misunderstood, it lacks the impact of face-to-face two-way communication, and it fails to adequately recognize efforts of members.

You recommend <u>solutions</u> to the problems you have identified and analyzed.

☐ Sometimes it is used to provide status on a long, drawn-out problem that is still being worked on. Not only will this keep management informed but it often generates renewed enthusiasm.

☐ The meeting area should be free from distractions.

Use a check list to assure that everything is ready. Typical items include: Extension cord, projector, screen, blackboard, chalk, etc.

☐ Set the room up ahead of time. Have your equipment in place and your charts ready to use.

☐ Place a name card in front of each person including members.

☐ Starting at the scheduled time makes a good impression.

PRESENTATION BY THE "SPOTLIGHTERS"
NOVEMBER 18, 1982
9:00 A.M.
ITEM   SPEAKER
• INTRODUCTION   MARY
• THEME   JOHN

Have an agenda that lists the sequence of items and the speakers. Each attendee should receive a copy.

☐ Introduce each member at the beginning of the presentation.

☐ As many members as possible should be involved as speakers.

☐ Each will be introduced immediately prior to speaking.

Have you ever had the feeling you were losing your audience? Perhaps your talk would come alive if you used visual aids.

Use charts that illustrate the techniques you have mastered such as Pareto and Cause-&-Effect. It helps to get your message across quickly and makes a good impression. Use charts, as is, that were prepared during the analysis rather than "Clean them up." It is simpler and adds a note of realism.

☐ Presentations can be made without any special aids. However, the effectiveness of the speaker can increase if certain equipment is utilized.

☐ It can be as basic as a blackboard.

☐ An overhead projector can eliminate the need to make large charts. It is a simple machine process to transfer your notes and small charts to a transparency that can be projected onto a large screen.

☐ A slide projector can also be used to aid in your presentation.

Flip charts allow the room to remain brightly illuminated while your material is presented.

☐ Flip charts have another advantage if you use it. Arrange for a member to hang the sheets on the wall as you finish with each. Thus, they can be referred to by you or your audience as needed.

☐ Make absolutely certain that everyone in the room can read your charts. Few things will turn off your audience as chart wording that's too small to read.

Translate words into graph form and you will save your audience both frustration and time in understanding your message. Pictures excell over words alone almost every time.

STOP THE A-V

Ask: What presentation aids have previously been used by members?

Answer: Various (including above).

☐ There is a variety of charts and graphs that can be helpful.

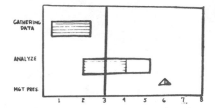

The milestone chart is an effective method to schedule and monitor activities.

☐ Line graphs are popular because of the ease with which they can be constructed.

☐ Bar charts are familiar to us, also.

Pie charts visually depict the portions which make up the whole.

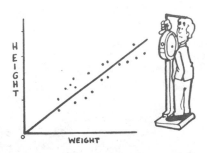

Scatter diagrams graphically display the relationship between two kinds of data. The pattern formed by the dots provides clues that can be interpreted.

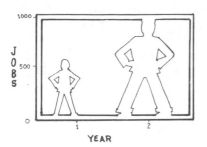

A pictograph like this, can mislead. It implies that production has quadrupled when in fact it has only doubled. The integrity of the user may well be questioned.

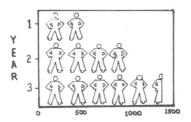

Here you have the advantages of the pictograph without the danger of misleading your audience. The final year demonstrates the use of a partial symbol.

General words such as "pet" evoke different reactions from people. Use care to be as specific as possible so as to prevent misunderstanding.

☐ Use your agenda to set the direction for the course of your presentation and stay on it. Avoid distractions if you can.

Want to get your message across? Talk their language! Express achievements in such things as schedule, quality, cost, and safety.

☐ The KISS principle: Keep It Sweet and Simple. One highly successful executive practiced his presentations on younger members of his family to assure his speech was understandable and that he could capture and hold their attention.

Bring an example of the actual hardware or paper and at the appropriate time let the audience handle and examine it. Few things work more effectively to clearly get your message across.

☐ If necessary, have everyone adjourn to the work area to witness the changes, or proposed changes, first-hand.

☐ If a tour to the area is impractical, show photographs or slide photos.

Distribute handouts too early and the audience may decide that the material is more interesting than the speaker.

☐ Be proud of your achievements. Talk about them. Your audience wants to hear about your victories.

Here is a question for you. Your team has failed to solve an important problem and has decided to move on. Should you make a presentation to report on the failure? Of course. Edison conducted over 3,000 experiments trying to build the light bulb. Rather than 3,000 failures, he said he had 3,000 victories because each test moved him closer to success.

Thank those who have helped you. It makes you look good. They look good. And the trust to assure a continued "win-win" cooperation is established.

To what level of management should the presentation be made? To the manager to whom the leader reports.

STOP THE A-V

> *Ask:*   *Why not make the presentation to higher level management.*
>
> *Answer:*   *The normal reporting channels must be used.*
>
> *Comment:*   *If projects are truly selected from within the work area of members, their manager is perfectly qualified to evaluate the recommendation.*

☐   Encourage questions to assure your message is understood. The more confident members may not wait. Rather, <u>they</u> may even direct questions <u>to</u> <u>the</u> <u>audience</u> to assure clear understanding.

 Let your enthusiasm come out. It's contagious! However, it is often easier said than done. We tend to tense up and inhibit our actions when speaking to an audience. The solution? Practice. Over exaggerate in practice and it becomes easy to let your natural enthusiasm show in public.

☐   A big smile relaxes both you and your audience and better allows your enthusiasm to come through.

Gestures can add impact and clarity to the communication process. Practice will help perfect your skill at doing this.

☐ Cue cards containing key words are a superb way to assure you will not forget portions of your talk.

Write your speech out word-for-word if you prefer. But, as you read it, look up frequently at your audience.

☐ A dry run prior to the presentation eases tensions and paves the way for a smoother and more effective presentation.

☐ Some members find it more comfortable to work in pairs during a presentation — a good way to build confidence!

What's the next project for your group? Usually, it has already begun. Before adjourning someone should provide a brief status report including a forecast of when it will be completed. Your manager will be impressed and it serves as a committment that will stimulate member activity.

☐ How frequently should a management presentation be made? As often as necessary but strive for every three months or so. Sometimes more than one project is covered during a single presentation.

☐ Everyone benefits from this remarkable communication process -- members, management, and the entire organization.

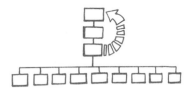

Do not use the presentation as a means of circumventing the normal chain of command so as to force a favorable response. That is not a win-win technique and will surely result in future problems.

Do not shock your manager by putting him on the spot with unexpected requests for solutions, funding, or manpower increases. No surprises, please!

The management presentation is a splendid opportunity for members to communicate their ideas and achievements to management. It is a rewarding experience for all.

NOTES

WORK SHEET

1. Imagine your team is preparing for a management presentation. It is likely that both the team, and the manager to whom the presentation will be made, will want others to attend.

    Assignment: Construct a list of all those who should attend as well as those who might be interested. Briefly indicate why in each case.

2. An agenda should be available to all attendees.

    Assignment: Construct an abreviated mock agenda. Use your imagination.

3. Occasionally a surprise occurs at a management presentation. You are speaking when a manager (an invited guest) says, "One of my engineers recommended that solution two years go, so what's new?" Everyone looks shocked.

<u>Assignment:</u> What do you respond?

QUIZ

1. Presentations should be done by:

   a. The leader only
   b. The leader and assistant leader
   c. The leader and members

2. Charts used in the presentation do not need to be professionally prepared.

   True_____   False_____

3. Presentations are used to make recommendations to management. Other reasons include:

   1._____
   2._____

4. Preferrably, the duration of the management presentation should be:

   a. About 30 minutes
   b. About 60 minutes
   c. Only what is necessary

5. Identify at least four kinds of charts and graphs.

   1._____
   2._____
   3._____
   4._____

6. Management presentations can highlight improvements, in several general categories. At least three of these are:

   1._____
   2._____
   3._____

7. The original Cause-&-Effect diagram normally becomes very messy as it is developed. It is recommended that it be neatly re-done and unnecessary clutter removed prior to the management presentation.

   True_____   False_____

8. The chairperson for a management presentation must always be the leader.

   True_____   False_____

9. Name at least two methods (in addition to charts) that help managment to clearly understand your presentation.

   1._____
   2._____

10. Should the leader introduce each speaker, or should each speaker introduce the next one?

    a.   The leader
    b.   Each speaker
    c.   Optional

11. An advantage of management presentations is that it allows us to invite higher level management and appeal directly to them for favorable decisions.

    True_____   False_____

12. A management presentation should begin at the time specified. One possible exception might be:

    _____
    _____

QUIZ ANSWERS

1.   The leader and members

2.   True

3.   1.   Present status of current projects.
      2.   Describe completed projects that
            did not need management approval.

4.   Only what is necessary.

5.   Expect a variety of responses such as:

      Line chart
      Bar graph
      Column graph
      Pie chart
      Scatter diagram
      Control chart
      Pareto chart
      Histogram

6.   Expect answers such as:

      Quality
      Schedule
      Costs
      Attitudes

7.   False.   Too often, the neatly redone chart
      loses its believability.

8.   False

9.   Answers may include:

      Actual hardware
      Photographs
      A tour

10. Optional

11. False. Do not use the management presentation to circumvent the normal channels.

12. Answers might include:

     * Your manager is late
     * A top executive has not arrived

In either event, it is probably wise to telephone the absent person's office before proceeding.

NINTH MEETING

Welcome the attendees.

Introduce the guests.

Read and approve the minutes of the last meeting.

Review and discuss the material on The Management Presentation, and re-do the quiz if helpful.

Discuss responses to the worksheet exercise.

Work on the current project.

Give assignments, if appropriate.

Post the project schedule and review it if necessary.

Suggest that the members be thinking about the next phase of the current project.

Announce the date, time, and place of the next meeting.

Thank attendees for their attention and cooperation.

Make sure the secretary prepares the minutes.

Confer with your facilitator, if required.

TENTH MEETING

Welcome members and guests.

Introduce any guests present.

Have the minutes of the last meeting read and approved.

Work on the current project.

Give assignments, if appropriate.

Post the project schedule and alter it, if necessary.

Suggest that members be thinking about the next phase of the current project.

Announce the date, time, and place of the next meeting.

Thank the attendees for their attention and cooperation.

Make sure the secretary prepares the minutes.

Confer with your facilitator if required.

NOTES

AN ON-GOING ACTIVITY

The tenth meeting was the first one held without devoting time to training, if you followed the suggested agendas; but, as time passes either you or one or more of the members will feel the need to repeat the A-Vs. The second and subsequent times around will result in picking up more information, more reality, and a clearer understanding of each technique.

Some "old timers" say that, after a period of time, a change often takes place. The format of a "meeting" is gradually replaced with a well-organized team activity. "It operates like a beautifully designed and smooth-running machine," they say. At some point, this may happen to your group, too.

It is probable, as your team "matures," that the members will need and want more advanced training, such as in the use of Histograms, $\overline{X} \bullet R$ Charts, NP Control Charts, Stratification, and more. These advanced training materials are published by the Quality Circle Institute.

INDIVIDUAL GROUP ACCOMPLISHMENTS

Name *"Impactors"*

Date Started	Leader	Project Description	Date Completed	Savings or Result
3-17-79	Jones	Broken cases - cause unknown. Investigation showed cause due to "jarring" due to machine handling. Bumper cushions installed at cost of $140.	4-9-79	$3,240
4-2-79	Jones	Malfunction of circuit breaker units. Cause due to excessive heat from use of Type K Solder guns.	4-30-79	8,660

This form is maintained by the facilitator or leader. It is an on-going record of one groups', achievements. It does more than inform others of accomplishments -- it informs the leader and members how well they are doing. As each new item is added, see that (among others) the facilitator receives a copy.

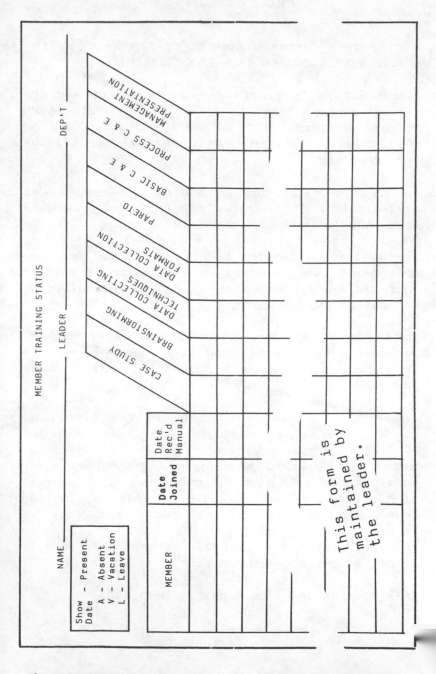

MEMBER TRAINING STATUS

NAME _____ LEADER _____ DEP'T _____

Show – Present
Date
A – Absent
V – Vacation
L – Leave

MEMBER	Date Joined	Date Rec'd Manual	CASE STUDY	BRAINSTORMING	DATA COLLECTING TECHNIQUES	DATA COLLECTION FORMATS	PARETO	BASIC C & E	PROCESS C & E	MANAGEMENT PRESENTATION

This form is maintained by the leader.

PROJECT SUMMARY

The Project Summary Report is prepared by the leader with guidance from the facilitator.

Essentially, it records the team project and the various actions taken to solve it. Indicate which persons and organizations were contacted and on what dates. Describe what analysis techniques were employed.

Answer the questions regarding the management presentation, the manager's acceptance or rejection, and implementation data.

In the section labeled RESULTS, list any measureable gains such as error rate decrease, scrap and waste fall-offs, decrease in customer complaints, and dollar improvements.

In the same section, make note of attitude improvements as reflected by such items as reduced absenteeism, turnover, and other morale-type indicators.

The audit summary should be done by a neutral party -- perhaps someone in an official cost evaluation group, maybe done by the same person or group that evaluates employee suggestions. The auditor should be able to depend on cost information entered on the back side of this form by the leader, members, facilitator, and others.

The facilitator, and probably others, will receive a copy of the completed form.

This form is shown on Pages 247 and 248.

PROJECT SUMMARY

_____   _____   _____
    Circle Name   Organization   Leader

Title of Project _____
_____

Date Started _____   Date Completed _____

Summary of Actions Taken   (Include individuals, organizations, dates, etc.)

DATE OF MGMT. PRESENTATION _____ ACCEPTED? _____ IMPLEMENTED? _____
If not accepted, why not?

_____

RESULTS:
Measurable (Work related):

Attitude Improvements:

_____

AUDIT SUMMARY   (Work sheet of savings & expenses on back side)

                    Total Estimated Savings $ _____

                    Total Costs   _____

                    Savings   _____

_____   _____   _____ _____
    Auditor   Organization   Telephone   Date

PROJECT SUMMARY
Work Sheet

VARIOUS ESTIMATED COSTS as determined by Circle Leader, members, facilitator, etc.

Total
Costs

ESTIMATED SAVINGS as calculated by the Circle leader, members, facilitator, etc.

Total
Savings

COMMENTS